First Printing: 2025
ISBN 978-1-954158-41-2

I0459385

Humorist Books is an imprint of *Weekly Humorist* owned and operated by
Humorist Media LLC.

Weekly Humorist is a weekly humor publication, subscribe online at
weeklyhumorist.com

99 Wall Street #2012 New York, NY 10005
weeklyhumorist.com - humoristbooks.com - humoristmedia.com

Edited by Brian Boone
Book design by Marty Dundics

This is a work of fiction. Names, characters, businesses, places, events, locales,
and incidents are either the products of the author's imagination or used in a
fictitious manner, except in cases when public figures and events are being
satirized through fictionalized depictions and/or personality paro- dies
(permitted under Hustler Magazine v. Fallwell, 485 US 46, 108 S.Ct 876, 99
L.E.2d 41 (1988)). Any resemblance to actual persons, living or dead, or actual
events is purely coincidental.

HUMORIST
BOOKS
New York

How to Succeed in Academia

(While Failing at Everything Else)

By Ross Bullen

YOU GOT THIS
Student Loan Debt, High Blood Pressure, and a 1995 Toyota Tercel

Are you passionate about learning, teaching, and making less than $15,000 a year? Do you enjoy tweed blazers, crisp autumn afternoons, and stealing lunch from unattended cafeteria trays? Have you ever longed to drive, sleep, and hold your office hours in a 30-year-old car? If so, then a career in academia might be right for you!

"But wait," you ask, "how can someone like me break into a field as prestigious and rarefied as academia?"

First of all, you need to understand that academics never ask each other questions this directly. If you want to fit in, you should try something like:

"I have a question that is more of a comment."

Or, "I have a two-part question. And one of those parts has two parts, so it's really three questions." You should then ask no fewer than seven questions, none of which have anything to do with what the other person was talking about.

Or, "I know I was on my phone the whole time you were talking, but I'd still like to deliver a 12-minute, uninterrupted monologue about how everything you said was wrong."

Second, you should know that this is not how books work. I'm writing these words *long before* you are reading them, so it's not like this is a conversation. If you're just learning this fact about how books work now, you're probably not cut out for a career in academia. Sorry.

Likewise, if you're the kind of person who genuinely enjoys a good conversation, you're probably not going to enjoy working in academia either, unless you think asking "so what are you working on these days?" and then ignoring everything the other person says counts as a good conversation. If that sounds like a deal breaker for you, close this book right now, place it back on your bookshelf, and immediately purchase several more copies of this very same book to see if one of them works out better for you.[1]

"But wait," you ask, "who are you to tell me what career I should choose?"

Good question. Although most books, including this one, feature an author biography that answers all of that, we've already established that books are scary and new for you, so I'll help you out with this. My name is Ross Bullen. I've worked at a beer bottle factory, a small-town Renaissance Faire, and a McDonald's across the street from a maximum-security prison. I've also spent the past two decades teaching off – sometimes *way* off – the tenure-track. And I can attest from personal experience that getting shafted by the Ivory Tower hurts just as badly as it sounds.

For those who don't know, "tenure-track" means a job where you are expected to receive tenure, i.e., a job for life, unless of course you work in Florida, West Virginia, or [INSERT NAME OF LATEST REPUBLICAN-RULED NIGHTMARE STATE HERE]. The typical tenure-track career path is Assistant Professor, Associate Professor, Full Professor – at which point you can either become a Dean, a Vice-President, or Jordan Peterson (disclaimer: none of these options are healthy or endorsed by the author). The problem is that the number of tenure-track jobs has been declining steadily for the past 40 years.[2] These days, most professors work

---

[1] I'm still counting on you not knowing how books work.

[2] Despite this fact, almost every graduate student will encounter a tenured professor who tells them that there will be a wave of faculty retirements and a rush of new tenure-track jobs in the next few years. There actually was a story in the *New York Times* about this, which is probably what your professor is remembering. It was published in 1989. By that same logic, I'm predicting that East Germany will win a silver medal in shot put at the next Summer Olympics, and that *Mr. Belvedere* will become the longest-running sitcom of all time.

Fig. 1. How the Tenure-Track Works

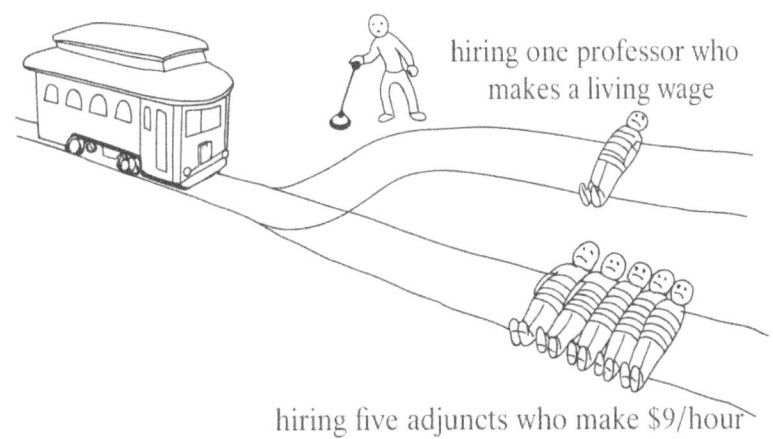

hiring one professor who makes a living wage

hiring five adjuncts who make $9/hour

jobs with weird titles like LTA (Limited-Term Appointment), VAP (Visiting Assistant Professor), or RACCOONS (Rejected At Community Colleges Or Other Nice Schools). But the majority of college teachers are what's known as "adjunct professors."[3]

---

[3]NOTE ON TERMINOLOGY / NOTE SUR LA TERMINOLOGIE

In addition to experiencing all the indignities associated with being a middle-aged, largely unsuccessful, non-tenure track professor, the author of this book also has to grapple with the bonus indignity of being Canadian. The means the author must constantly translate Canadian academic jargon into "American" for his dozens and dozens of readers from the United States. This isn't as simple as just removing the letter "u" from various words, though it does pain the author to see a beautiful world like "colour" pared down to "color" just because James Madison declared war on the letter "u" (and the British Empire) during the War of 1812. Another clear sign that I am Canadian, and not American, is that I went out of my way to bring up the War of 1812. Nor is it as simple as avoiding perfectly good words like "toque," "chesterfield," and "universal health care" just because these concepts are offensive to the American palate. Unfortunately, academia has its own rarefied jargon, which is every bit as complicated as it is unnecessary and useless. So, for the interested reader, here is a complete-ish guide to all the academic terms I use in this book that have been translated from the maple-dipped magic of Canadian English:

ADJUNCT PROFESSOR: This term is sometimes used in Canada, but it is much more common for Canadian schools to refer to adjuncts as "sessionals." The origin of this term is controversial, though many believe it comes from low alcohol, "sessional" beer. Just like you could drink one regular beer or 3-4 sessional beers, you could hire one regular/tenured professor or 3-4 sessional professors (okay, more like 15 sessional professors) for the same amount of money. You get more bang for your buck, although in both cases you are also arguably getting a watered down and ultimately disappointing version of the real thing. Harsh? Yes. I recommend you cope with this brutal reality by drinking 3-4 (okay, more like 15) beers. And no, not the sessional ones.

CHAIRS: Department chairs are fairly common in Canada, though some schools use the term "Department head," which has the immediate effect of a) conveying a sense of authority and b) making everybody think about oral sex when they really, really don't want to.

MONEY: Every time I mention money, just imagine that it is worth 60 cents on the dollar and that it has a picture of this fucking guy on it:

PRESIDENT / VICE-PRESIDENT / ETC: No, Canadian universities don't have "Prime Ministers" instead of "Presidents," but they do sometimes add an extra term like "Vice-Chancellor" to the President's title, lending them a sense of gravitas, and also making them sound like a visiting dignitary from the Klingon home world.

STARBUCKS / DUNKIN' / ETC: Most American coffee places have a presence in Canada, but if you want to add a dash of Canadian realism to this book, replace all such references with Tim Hortons. Replace all mention of "venti" or "grande" with "double double," a style of coffee named after its immediate effect on both your heart rate and chances of suddenly dying. Donuts holes are Timbits. A breakfast sandwich is a breakfast sandwich, except in Quebec, where it's a "Timatin" for some fucking reason. (In solidarity with my unilingual American comrades, I am refusing to learn what "matin" means.)

6

The original idea behind adjunct professors makes sense: Sometimes schools needed an outside expert to teach a class in a niche area, and even though this expert usually had another job, the school still paid them a stipend for their trouble. So far, so good. The problem is that once colleges realized they *could* hire professors on the cheap, they decided they *should always do this*. And although a handful of new tenure-track professors get hired each year, most people teaching at colleges in the U.S. (and elsewhere) do so as adjuncts. The typical adjunct professor career path is Adjunct, Adjunct, Unemployed, Subway Sandwich Artist™, Adjunct. Technically, tenure-track professors get paid for research and service in addition to teaching, and adjuncts don't, but that just means that adjuncts wind up doing research and service for free. (how else are you supposed to prove that you're worthy of a tenure-track job, should one ever become available?)

FAMOUS ADJUNCTS IN HISTORY: No. 17

ABRAHAM LINCOLN

Until 1900, Presidents were paid a nominal salary of one sack of tobacco per full moon. Lacking family wealth, Lincoln was forced to take a second job teaching freshman business communication at a D.C.-area community college, and a third job selling ethnic food (sandwiches) outside the White House. Luckily, his upbringing in a poorly-heated log cabin prepared him for the working conditions of most adjunct professors in the 19th century (and the 20th and 21st centuries). When he died, he left behind his wife, two sons, a grieving nation, and 57 ungraded essays on "leadership and conflict resolution."

Courtesy West Wing Community College
Faculty Profile Web Page

If all of this sounds bad, that's because it is. But this book is not called *How to Avoid Working in Academia* (although if anybody has a book like that, please, for the love of God, send it to me ASAP). It's *How to Succeed in Academia*, and that's just what I'm going to teach you to do. This book will guide you through every step of your academic journey, whether it's finishing your dissertation on time (or at least before the heat death of the universe), applying for an academic job (by summoning the ancient Mesopotamian demon Pazuzu), or overcoming imposter syndrome (even if you're a family of raccoons living in a Fjällräven Parka).

So, grab a seat, a nice mug of warm milk, and settle in for some good old fashioned book reading (at least until your shift at Subway starts). You're an academic now!

Fig. 2. Tenure-Track Jobs vs. Belief in Magic Beans

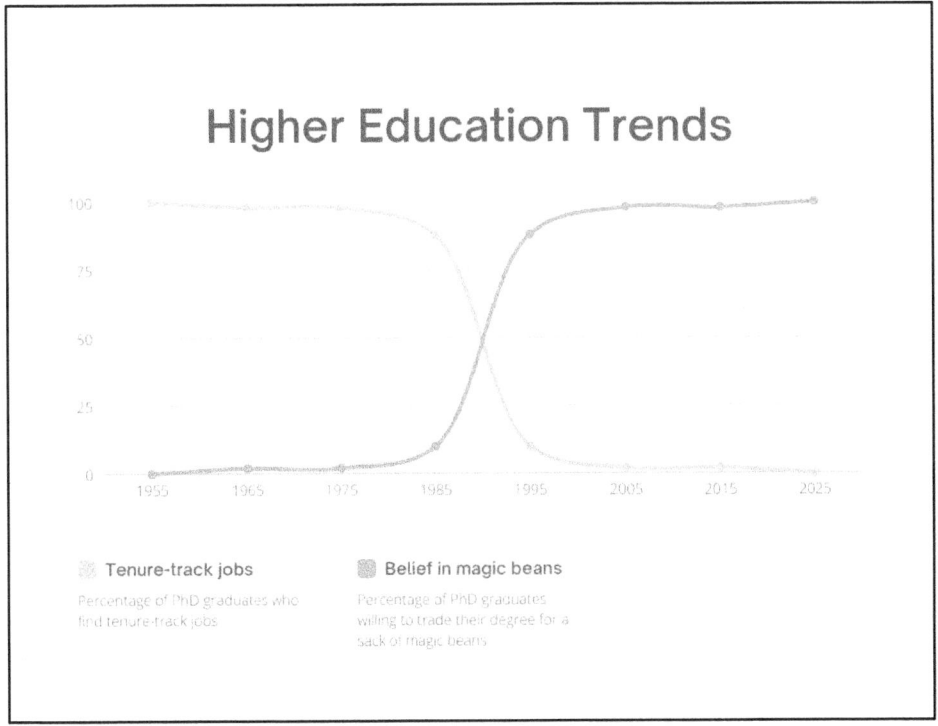

HOW TO USE THIS BOOK

Read it slowly from start to finish.

Read it quickly starting from the last page for that quick "just finished a book" hit.

Read it backwards and upside down as a fun conversation starter on public transit.

Prop it under the leg of a table, a desk, or a child with a weird gait.

Shred each page into long strips, ¼ inch thick. Boil a large pot of salted water. While water boils, heat olive oil, garlic, and chili flakes in a sauté pan. When garlic becomes fragrant, add one can of crushed San Marzano tomatoes. Simmer at medium low heat. Add strips of *How to Succeed in Academia* to boiling water and cook 6 minutes until *al dente*. Strain strips of book, toss with tomato sauce, and a generous handful of Pecorino Romano. Season to taste with salt and pepper and throw the whole disgusting mess in the fucking garbage. Thanks a lot for ruining my book, asshole. You'd better buy another copy, or I'll hunt you down. *Buon appetito!*

If lost in the woods, use this book as kindling.

Alternatively, eat this book, following the recipe above.

Or just eat it raw, it won't kill you.

If it does kill you, at least you'll be alone in the woods and this probably won't create any legal trouble for the author or the publisher, which we appreciate.

Rip out each page, rearrange them, and see if that book is more helpful for you. If it is, you need to pay the author and publisher for a second copy. This is the law, so make sure you do it. Don't look up the specific law or anything, just send cash in an envelope before you get in even more trouble (we already know you illegally destroyed a book).

Cut out each individual word in the book to create a series of threatening notes demanding money from strangers. If anyone pays up, the author and publisher are once again entitled to a healthy cut of the proceeds.

Assign it as part of your college syllabus.

Assign it as part of your highly popular and influential book club (send this one to Reese Witherspoon, lol!).

Just slide a copy under Reese Witherspoon's front door is what I'm saying.

Seriously, go break into Reese Witherspoon's house right now even if you have to hop a fence or strangle a guard dog. Do it. DO IT.

Assign a copy to your cell block reading group as you round out a fun and breezy nine-year sentence for stalking Reese Witherspoon.

A few copies duct taped around your torso will make you 100% shiv proof as well. Just saying.

Line a litter box with this book, paper train a puppy, or just take a shit on it all by yourself.

Use this book to discover that you are a great artist! In the space below, please draw your best artistic interpretation of "academic success." Send a photo of your entry to ross.daniel.bullen@gmail.com. The winning entry will be used as the book's cover image when it is reissued as a Norton Critical Edition. Good luck!

CHAPTER I:
Your Undergraduate Years

Welcome to college! Remember, you earned this through years of hard work and hitting the books every single day. Unless, of course, you happen to be rich, your parents happen to be extremely rich, you are a legacy admission to an Ivy League school (in which case, everybody you've ever met is rich), you have the God-given ability to throw a football 75 yards, or you're an undercover FBI agent trying to infiltrate a cadre of campus radicals who turn out to be a group of grad students who meet once a month to read *Das Kapital* and drink chamomile tea. For everybody else, you deserve to be here for the best four years of your life, or until your tuition money runs out, whichever comes first. But it's not going to be easy.

Luckily, this book has got you covered. This chapter will teach you everything you need to know to get the most out of your undergraduate years, beginning with the most important questions of all: *Does the author of this book accept cash gifts via PayPal?* As is the case with all non-tenured professors, the answer is yes, do with that information what you will. And now for the second most important question: *Just what is a university, anyway?*

The modern university has three core missions: the first is to make money by turning most of its campus into a paid parking lot; the second is to make even more money by charging students the equivalent rent as a three-bedroom apartment for an Ikea SLÄKT bedframe in a tiny shared room; the third is to give everybody's life purpose and meaning each March by making the world's most talented basketball players play a must-watch televised tournament for free. But believe it or not, in ancient times the university's core mission was related to education.

Fig. 3. The Modern University

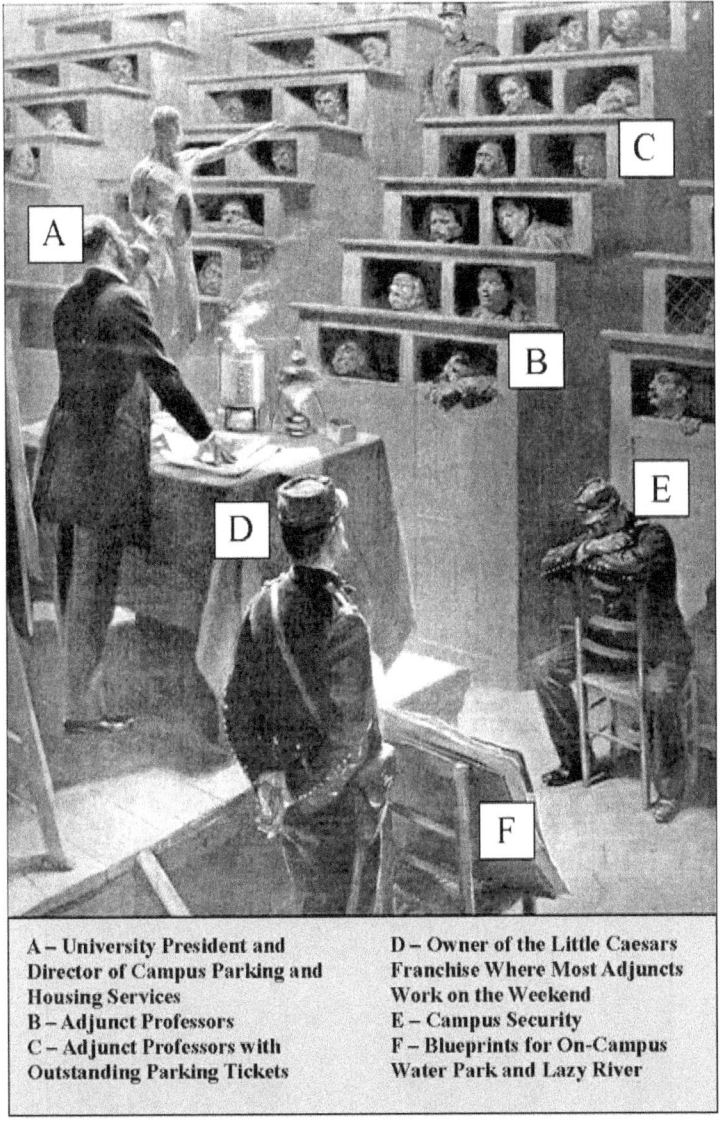

A – University President and Director of Campus Parking and Housing Services
B – Adjunct Professors
C – Adjunct Professors with Outstanding Parking Tickets
D – Owner of the Little Caesars Franchise Where Most Adjuncts Work on the Weekend
E – Campus Security
F – Blueprints for On-Campus Water Park and Lazy River

The first university was founded in Athens, Greece in the year 387 B.C.E. by the philosopher Plato. Plato's teacher, Socrates, wandered from place to place, argued with strangers, made no money, overstayed his welcome at parties, and drank too much cheap wine, which has led some scholars to identify him as history's first adjunct professor. Plato was determined to make a different kind of career for himself. His first move was to write down all of Socrates' good ideas and publish them under his own name, thereby inaugurating the great academic tradition of tenured scholars taking credit for work done by adjuncts and grad students. Plato's second move was to start his own university, which he called "The Academy." Plato's initial plan for The Academy was to get rich by charging students 30 drachmas per day to stable their donkeys in his olive grove/parking lot, but before long he realized that he could charge them even more money if he actually pretended to teach them something.

Fig. 4. Plato Explaining His Latest Tuition Hike to His Student Aristotle

Plato's best student was a brilliant young philosopher named Aristotle, and naturally Plato offered him a lucrative contract as an adjunct professor, including 25% off donkey parking fees and one handful of raw olives per week. But Aristotle had a better idea and invented one of the pillars of modern higher education: giving out vanity degrees to the children of the rich and powerful. In Aristotle's case, his student was the son of King Philip II of Macedonia, a sprightly and surprisingly violent young lad named Alexander.[4] Just like today's Ivy League-trained scientists who use their education (and a CIA slush fund) to make the world a better place by inventing wonderful things like Agent Orange and the Hellfire R9X Missile, Alexander used Aristotle's lessons in science, philosophy, and ethics to conquer the entire known world and kill thousands of people along the way. Tragically, Alexander died at the age of 32 after drinking a vat of wine poisoned by adjunct professors who were angry about the low salary and non-existent benefits at Macedonian Empire University (Babylon Campus).

The university as we know it today first appeared in Ancient Rome under the leadership of Gaius Julius Caesar, *Dictator Perpetuo* and Vice-President of Student Services. Caesar established many practices that are still widespread in higher education, including the founding of unsuccessful satellite campuses in far-flung cultural backwaters like France and England, hiring and/or executing adjunct professors based on a simple thumbs up, thumbs down system, and providing adjuncts with part-time jobs at a pizza restaurant to help bring their annual income within spitting distance of the poverty line. This restaurant, known today as Little Caesars, while no longer owned by a university, is still staffed exclusively by adjunct professors, grad students, and managers (teenagers). Despite these important innovations, Caesar drew the ire of many people in academia, and in 44 B.C.E. he was assassinated by a loose alliance of hired mercenaries, political enemies, and students angered by recent price increases for HOT-N-READY Pizza®at on-campus Little Caesars locations.

And so, from the collective genius of Plato, Aristotle, and the first guy to melt cheese on bread and charge people $30 for it, the modern university was born. We will learn more about the history of the university in subsequent chapters, but now it's time for something that usually has no place in academia: useful and practical advice. It is our

---

[4]Later in life Alexander would change his name from "Alexander of Macedon, B.A. (Interdisciplinary Studies)" to the admittedly more impressive "Alexander the Great."

sincere hope that the following "how to" guides help you get through your undergraduate years with great memories, a robust GPA, and enough student debt to haunt you well into middle age.

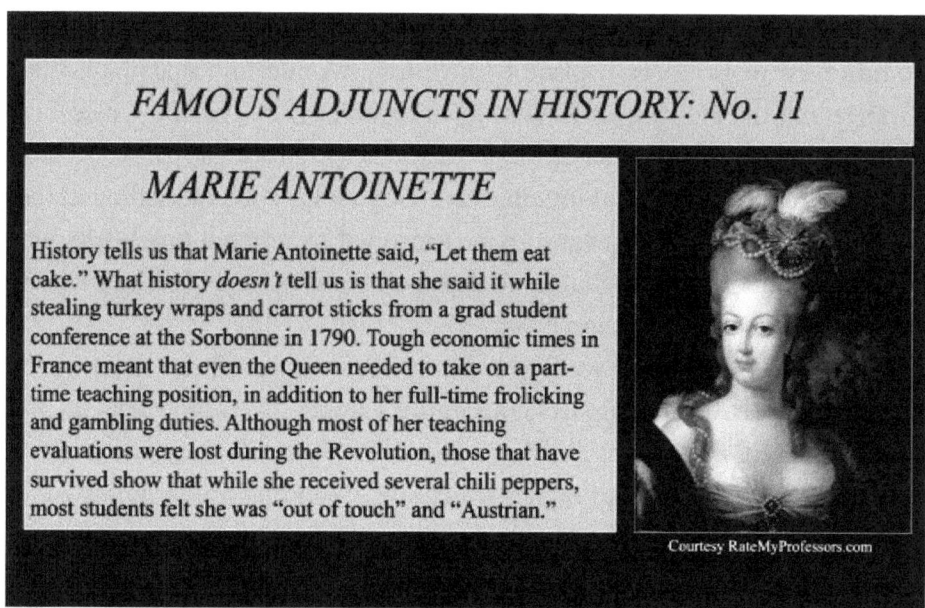

FAMOUS ADJUNCTS IN HISTORY: No. 11

MARIE ANTOINETTE

History tells us that Marie Antoinette said, "Let them eat cake." What history *doesn't* tell us is that she said it while stealing turkey wraps and carrot sticks from a grad student conference at the Sorbonne in 1790. Tough economic times in France meant that even the Queen needed to take on a part-time teaching position, in addition to her full-time frolicking and gambling duties. Although most of her teaching evaluations were lost during the Revolution, those that have survived show that while she received several chili peppers, most students felt she was "out of touch" and "Austrian."

Courtesy RateMyProfessors.com

How to Email Your Professor

Life in academia involves a lot of email. It can be tough to know the dos and don'ts of emailing your professor, so hopefully this guide clears up some of the confusion.

Step One: Finding Your Professor's Email Address

This seems like it should be relatively straightforward, but it can be surprisingly complicated. The first thing you should do is Google your prof. If you find a faculty website with a picture of your professor and a list of publications and degrees, they are probably on the tenure-track, and you can just use whatever email address is listed on their profile. This is the best-case scenario. Consider yourself lucky! In the coming decades, as tenure is gradually eliminated, this memory will become as quaint and distant as sending someone a telegram or riding one of those old-timey bicycles with one gigantic wheel. (If your professor sends telegrams or rides one of those bicycles, they definitely have tenure, and definitely don't check their email. Get in touch via office hours, telegram, or a haunted raven who interrupts them during a midnight reverie.)

Step Two: Finding Your Adjunct Professor's Email Address

Welcome to the Wild Fucking West. This is by far the likeliest outcome, so you might think you can plan for it, but – believe me – *nothing* can prepare you for the maelstrom of chaos and confusion that is about to engulf you. Once again, start with Google. This time, instead of a coherent and easily searchable webpage, you will find your professor's name listed on the website of no fewer than six different universities (none of which are yours), on a ten-year-old program for an academic conference held in Moose Jaw, Saskatchewan, and as the recipient of Subway's Sandwich Artist™ of the Month Award for October. All social media will be locked down because your professor is worried about search committees finding a photo of them holding a beer five years ago. Keep digging.

Step Three: Finding Friendster

Among the detritus of the internet, you find what seems to be a kind of ancient social media profile for someone who bears a passing resemblance to your professor. Unlike their Facebook, Instagram, Twitter, etc., this one isn't private, but it also hasn't been updated since 2003. It's something called "Friendster," and unless you were born between 1975 and 1985, you will have no idea what that is.[5] You try to sign up to "friend" your professor, but you quickly discover that Friendster went bankrupt during the Obama administration. This will require some creative thinking, which is exactly the kind of thing you'd like to ask your professor to help you with if you could get in touch with them, but you can't, so you ask ChatGPT instead.

---

[5]If you were born between 1975 and 1985, congratulations on returning to school! In retrospect, dropping out to audition for *Survivor* probably wasn't the greatest life strategy, but at least now you can get an objectively worse education for only four times the tuition.

Step Four: Finding Your Adjunct Professor at American Apparel
ChatGPT is still a work in progress, but after some back and forth it not only tells you that you need to use a time machine to reach your professor, it provides you with step-by-step instructions for *building* that time machine. You're skeptical, but you purchase all the necessary components, flip a switch, and before you know it you emerge from a bright fog into a crisp autumn morning in the year 2003. Things feel different here. No smartphones. No self-driving cars mangling random pedestrians. You eventually learn that you will need to access the internet via something known as an "internet café." At the café you learn that you will need to "dial up" the internet and – even stranger – you will need to use something called "cash" to pay for this service. After making the necessary arrangements, you hop on Friendster and discover that your professor works somewhere called "American Apparel." Using an ancient text that the internet café guy calls a "phone book," you locate the nearest American Apparel store and decide to check it out.

Step Five: Finding Some Answers (And a Zip-Up Hoodie)
The American Apparel store is weird. It seems to consist solely of overpriced 1980s gym clothing and softcore pornography. Trying to remain incognito, you put on an oversize zip-up hoodie. Through the drawstring-tightened hood you catch a glimpse of someone who looks like your professor folding tube socks next to a cash register. You try to sneak closer, but you trip over a cardboard box full of neon pink leggings. Your professor rushes over to help you up. They ask if you need anything else, at which point you ask them for an extension on an assignment that is due more than twenty years in the future. Your professor is obviously confused by this, so you explain it all, telling them that twenty something years from now they will make $12,000 a year to teach Intro to Sociology to a lecture hall full of bored teenagers. Your professor stares at the wall in dead-eyed silence for the next thirty minutes. They blink slowly and ask to see the time machine you used to get here. You show them the device, and no sooner have you explained the basics than your professor grabs it from you and announces that they would prefer to live out the rest

of their days as a Medieval peasant. They disappear in a flash of light and smoke. You do not have another time machine. It looks like you are stuck in 2003. You stumble out of the American Apparel, taking the hoodie with you.

Finding Your Fortune

There are lots of ways you could get rich in the past. Betting on the Super Bowl. Becoming an early investor in Facebook. But you stumble upon something even more lucrative. You track down all the future adjunct professors at your school and simply tell them what their life will look like two decades from now. Every single one of them grows silent for a long time and then immediately packs up a few belongings and leaves their current life behind. Some join monasteries. Some join the French Foreign Legion. In each case, though, they leave behind an apartment, a car or a bicycle, and other relics commonly possessed by future professors in the year 2003 (mostly *Buffy the Vampire Slayer* DVDs). All you have to do is sublet their apartments to other unwitting academics and sell their *Buffy* DVDs on something called "Craigslist." Before long you're bring in thousands of dollars each day. By the time you return to the year your assignment was due you're older, wiser, and way too rich to worry about going to college. Besides, your words of warning have had an effect. Every adjunct professor in America has ghosted on academia, and the few universities that have survived are staffed solely by a skeleton crew of tenured professors and A.I.-powered chatbots that were originally programmed to help customers select the right chicken sandwich at Popeye's. You wonder about the fate of your former professor who disappeared into the past and likely died of dysentery or the plague within a few weeks of their arrival. Remembering the haunted look on their face in American Apparel, you are confident that they would have no regrets.

How to Format Your Essay Using Any Style Guide

Most professors you encounter in college will want you to write an essay, and every one of them will want you to format that essay using a different style guide. It's confusing! Luckily, this guide will have you formatting your papers like a pro in no time at all.

Chicago Style

Print your essay and then spend the next two hours preparing a rich and zesty marinara sauce. Place your essay in a deep pie dish, cover it with a layer of sausage and cheese, top it off with your homemade red sauce, and throw it in a 425° oven for 35 minutes. Your essay is now finished! You have also guaranteed that nobody will ever like it (except for readers from the Chicago metropolitan area). If somebody says they like New York-Style essays better, include a footnote where you call them a "jag-off." If somebody tries to put ketchup on your essay, Chicago Style permits you to bury them alive under Wrigley Field.

APA Style

Before you begin writing, head to your local microbrewery and purchase a 12-pack of American Pale Ale (6% abv or higher). Return home and follow these 12 easy steps:

Step 1) Open a new Word document and open an APA. Ignore the Word document and drink the beer, followed by two more beers.

Step 2) Try to figure out how to include page numbers in your essay. Is it something in "Tools"? In "Format"? How did Bill Gates make $100 billion from this? Drink three more beers.

Step 3) Open a second Word doc for some reason. In lieu of writing, insert a picture of Captain Picard you found on the internet. Another beer? You bet.

Step 4) Go for a walk to clear your head. Make sure you take a beer with you. Hold on to the empty bottle in case you need to pee in the alley behind Taco Bell (NOTE: you will definitely need to pee in the alley behind Taco Bell).

Step 5) Take the last four beers to your futon while you watch just one episode of *Love Is Blind*. Just one.

Steps 6 through 9) NAP TIME.

Step 10) Wake up 12 hours later with your face stuck to your MacBook's keyboard. Send an email to your professor asking for an extension before puking in the paper bag you brought home from Taco Bell.

Step 11) Open a new Word document.

Step 12) Enter a 12-step program.

ASA Style

Ignore whatever topic you were assigned and write an essay about nineteenth-century baseball player Asa Brainard instead. Here are some possible "hooks" you might use to draw your reader in:

- Who became the starting ace for the Brooklyn Excelsiors after superstar pitcher Jim Creighton fatally injured himself while hitting a home run in 1862?
- Who made a whopping $1,100 pitching for the Cincinnati Red Stockings in 1869?
- Who is Major League Baseball's all-time home run leader? (NOTE: sometimes you should use a trick question to keep your readers on their toes)
- Who died of consumption in Denver, Colorado in 1888 at the ripe old age of 47?

After reading these fun facts about Asa Brainard your professor will forget all about the topic they originally assigned and give you a 78, which is, of course, the same number of walks Asa Brainard allowed between 1871 and 1874.

***Fig. 5. Popular Essay Topic/Nineteenth-Century
Baseball Player Asa Brainard***

Harvard Referencing

Just keep referencing the fact that you went to Harvard anytime anybody asks you about something you wrote, no matter how factually inaccurate it is. Eventually they'll just stop asking.

MLA Style

Throw your essay in a suitcase and catch the next flight to Malta International Airport (MLA). At MLA you meet your Airbnb host, Baldassar, who drives you to his country estate. Before long, you become lovers. You spend the late summer days wandering around Baldassar's organic vineyards, stopping occasionally to chat with local farmers. The farmers are friendly, but you notice that they fall quiet when you ask them how you should properly cite a YouTube video of Slavoj Žižek in your essay on the socio-ideological implications of *Vanderpump Rules*. You begin to wonder why you ever wanted to write such an essay in the first place, especially when you could spend each day watching the sun set into the azure sea while sipping from a jug of rustic wine instead.

Eventually, you release your essay, one page at a time, into the Mediterranean waters, while Baldassar rests his strong hand on your shoulder. Your "Works Cited" page is the last to float away.

Vancouver Style

Nobody has ever heard of this style, including people from Vancouver. Just do whatever the hell you want as long as it's double-spaced.

50 Fake Colleges You Can Use to Pad Your Resume

Sometimes it's easier to just skip college altogether. If you decide to go this route, simply toss one of these fake school names on your resume and nobody will be any the wiser.

1) Uranus University (Uranus, Missouri)
2) Gordon's Gator Wrangling Academy (Alligator, Mississippi)
3) Henrietta's Hooking Hall (Hooker, Oklahoma)
4) Tinpan Tinkering Tech (Hobo's Junction, Colorado)
5) Cumming College (Climax, Michigan)
6) McGill University (Montreal, Quebec)
7) Duloc College (Shrek's Corner, Arkansas)
8) Starfleet Academy (San Francisco, California)
9) Cheeseplate State (Cheesequake, New Jersey)
10) Cheesesteak State (Sandwich, Massachusetts)
11) Larry's Lawnmower Repair Shack (Cambridge, Massachusetts)
12) Dalhousie University (Halifax, Nova Scotia)
13) Manson University (Spahn Ranch, California)
14) Four Seasons Total Landscaping School of Media Relations (Philadelphia, Pennsylvania)
15) Ted Kaczynski Technology and Communications College (Lincoln, Montana)
16) Acme Corporation Academy (Taos, New Mexico)

17) Robert J. Gronkowski School of Brain Surgery and Rocket Science (Boston, Massachusetts)
18) McMaster University (Hamilton, Ontario)
19) Craptown College (Colon, Michigan)
20) Samuel S. Scrotum School of Business Management (Hackensack, New Jersey)
21) Merkin Academy (Bush Compound, Kennebunkport)
22) Hamburger University (Hamburg, Germany)
23) Ron DeSantis Splelling and Coutning amd Eductaion Academmy (Talahasey, Flarida)
24) Simon Fraser University (Vancouver, British Columbia)
25) Reuben College (Thousand Islands, New York)
26) Kazoo Academy (Kalamazoo, Michigan)
27) John Wick School of Conflict Resolution (New York, New York)
28) Doc Holliday Dental Academy (Tombstone, Arizona)
29) Old Burrito College (Uncertain, Texas)
30) Holy Mount University (Dildo, Newfoundland)
31) Tubthumper Academy (Chumbawumba, Oregon)
32) University of Regina (Regina, Saskatchewan)
33) St. Pete's Plumbing School (Flushing, Queens)
34) Carl Spackler Landscaping and Pest Removal Prep Academy (Bushwood Country Club, Nebraska)
35) IKEA HØME CØNSTRUCTIØN ÅND ÄNGER MÄNÅGEMENT ÄCÅDEMY (Stockholm, Sweden)
36) University of Western Ontario (London, Ontario)
37) Cola College (Soda Springs, Idaho)
38) Polyamory Polytechnic (Three Way, Tennessee)
39) Too Cool for School School (Cool, Texas)
40) Ass Academy (Buttzville, New Jersey)
41) Experimental Electricity and Biology College (Frankenstein, Missouri)
42) Popeyes Poultry Academy (Chicken, Alaska)
43) Ernie's Erotic Flower Arranging Academy (Humptulips, Washington)
44) University of Guelph (Guelph, Ontario)

45) Carmine's Charm School (Loveladies, New Jersey)

46) Harvard Business School (Satan's Kingdom, Massachusetts)

47) Yee Haw University (Yeehaw Junction, Florida)

48) Willie Nelson Agriculture Academy (Weed, California)

49) Mount Allison University (Sackville, New Brunswick)

50) Some Boring School (Boring, Oregon)

How to Attend a Campus Protest

Campus protests have been a hallmark of higher education since the 1960s. But you need to make sure you do it correctly or you might run the risk of minorly inconveniencing a senior academic administrator or a big donor! The following tips will help you rage against the machine while politely respecting the machine's right to crush you whenever it chooses.

Tip #1: Only Protest Stuff that Happened in the Past

Whenever possible, always try to protest something that happened at least 40 years ago. It's so easy to pick a side in the past because everyone agrees about which was the right one! In the past, Martin Luther King Jr. was a cuddly teddy bear beloved by everybody (except that one guy), Nelson Mandela was a hero who all white people (except from that one place) agreed should be free, and slavery was opposed by all white people (except for that one half of the country). See how easy it is to agree with stuff that happened in the past with a mere 40, 50, or 60 (or 160) years of hindsight? Civil Rights, the Vietnam War, South African apartheid: we were all on the same page about that stuff and we deserve a pat on the back for it. If you are considering protesting some modern-day injustice, ask yourself, "what will everybody think about this forty years from now?" And then, just to be sure, wait forty years before you say or do anything.

Tip #2: Don't Disturb Anybody

This is crucial. It's so important for you to get your message across without bothering or inconveniencing anybody. Ideally, they won't even see or hear you at all. In fact, just to be safe, you should probably stay at home. Don't post anything online, though. That could bother someone too. You can talk about it out loud, but only if nobody else is at home. If you have a cat at home, you should keep quiet, because any noise you make other than jiggling a bag of treats will annoy them. Dogs are okay, though. You can tell them all about it.

Tip #3: Don't Damage Property

You might not think that the glass vestibule of a bank branch is more valuable than the life of a child living in a refugee camp, but you would be wrong, wrong, wrong! Banks have hundreds of billions of dollars to their name, while starving children have virtually nothing (not even food!). So if you are angry that a bank – or any other corporation – is getting rich by selling weapons that are being used to kill children, don't smash a window, don't throw paint on a CEO, and certainly don't try to dissuade customers from giving them more money. It's important to remember that corporations are actually people, which means that they have feelings (and a team of corporate lawyers) too. Children are also people, of course, unless a bank, government, or weapons manufacturer says they aren't. Remember, in these situations, believing the person with the most money is always the morally correct choice.

Tip #4: Wear Sunscreen

No, it won't protect you from the tear gas and rubber bullets that your university president is going to send your way, but at least you won't get skin cancer.

ACADEMIC GLOSSARY

Easy A: As the name suggests, the easiest courses at every college start with letter "A." We recommend starting with Astrophysics and taking it from there.

Pledge Week: Using your favorite item from the Pledge family of home cleaning products, you will spend the week cleaning your adjunct professor's office, home, and car. Luckily for you, these are all the same thing.

Homecoming: In between paychecks, your adjunct professor may need to come stay at your home for a little while. Just leave out food, water, and a third-hand futon and they'll be fine.

Student Loans: It is a common practice for a professor to "loan" one of their students to another professor to help with education-related duties, including research, grading, and moving boxes of expensive wedding china out of their ex-wife's basement in the middle of the night.

Spring Break: That fun time of year when your adjunct professor realizes they aren't going to get any of the tenure-track jobs they applied for and their spirit slowly breaks. You should probably get out of their hair for a week or so, ideally by attending a foam party in Miami Beach.

GPA: Probably some kind of strong, tasty beer? Purchase a six-pack for your adjunct professor just to be sure. Maybe also buy them some groceries and a new pair of shoes while you're at it.

Academic Probation: Most people who work in academia are doing it at the behest of a probation officer who oversees their community service sentence for urinating in the university president's koi pond.

Quiz: Should I Apply to Grad School?

Question 1: How many Ivy League schools feature a dining hall named after one of your wealthy ancestors?
  a) 1-3
  b) 4-6
  c) my lawyers have advised me not to answer this question
  d) nobody in my family has been to an Ivy League school or a dining hall before

Question 2: What do you think is a reasonable starting salary for someone with an undergraduate degree?
  a) $100,000+
  b) $50,000-$99,999
  c) $15,000-$49,999
  d) $4/hour for grading essays + 10% discount at the on-campus Chipotle

Question 3: How do you like to spend your free time?
  a) nice dinners with friends
  b) off-the-beaten-path vacations
  c) driving the BMW your parents gave you for graduation
  d) fighting pigeons for day old bagels while waiting for your interlibrary loans to arrive

Question 4: ABD stands for...?
  a) "all but dissertation"
  b) "abnormal brain disease"
  c) "aggressive bragging disorder"
  d) all of the above

Question 5: My greatest source of happiness is...?
  a) family and friends
  b) spiritual and/or religious beliefs
  c) professional and financial success

d) delivering a twenty-minute monologue about how happiness is a "social construct" to horrified strangers at parties

ANSWER KEY: If you answered a, b, c, or d to *any* of these questions, you are obviously a huge nerd who loves tests, and you will go to grad school even if everybody tells you not to. Proceed to the next chapter!

CHAPTER II:
Grad School

For most people, the end of their undergraduate degree will be the end of their time in academia. They will graduate, get a shitty job, get a slightly better job, get married, have kids, have an open marriage, get therapy, get divorced, get custody of their kids every other weekend, and get their life back on track by taking advice from a guy who only consumes salt, raw beef, and amphetamines. It's really as simple as that. But for a select few unfortunate souls, the siren song of academia will only get louder (though this could be tinnitus from listening to Spotify's "This is Norwegian Black Metal" playlist while sitting through four years of undergrad lectures). These people are the future grad students of the world.

So what is a grad student anyway? Look, in the same way that nobody picks up a book called *How to Break Your Deepfake Pornography Addiction* unless they are already watching a distressing number of videos with titles like "Taylor Swift takes EVERY INCH of Shrek," you don't buy a book like this one unless you're already overeducated, underpaid, and maybe a little curious about what other sexually explicit Shrek videos you can find on the internet. But, just for the record, there *are* several advantages to going to grad school:

- The thrill of telling strangers you are a doctor.
- The thrill of disappointing strangers when you explain that you are a PhD not an MD.
- The thrill of crushing strangers' souls when you start telling them about your dissertation.
- Delaying most elements of normal adult life until at least your mid-30s.

- Permanently stopping relatives from asking you about your job after only one Thanksgiving dinner argument about the 1971 Chomsky-Foucault debate.
- Cyclical fashion trends means that impoverished grad student aesthetic will be cool every 15-20 years (bonus points if you stay in school that whole time).
- Ease of access to unattended snack trays at most on-campus events.

Okay, so you know what a grad student is, and some of the (extremely limited) benefits of being one. *But where did grad students come from?* This is a question that requires a deep dive through the historical record, so strap on your Walmart brand reading glasses and get ready to do some research (the real kind, not the kind where you go to the library and fall asleep in a study carrel for four hours).

The first graduate students appeared in China around the year 500 B.C.E., during the "Spring and Autumn period" (named after the two times of year when grad students were traditionally offered a single coin in payment for their services). Although wandering and impoverished scholars were a common sight in pre-imperial China, it was the philosopher Kong Qiu – or Confucius – who formalized their place in Chinese society.[6] Confucius's philosophy emphasized morality, responsibility, mass education, and tricking young people into spending their 20s in abject poverty to write a 300-page dissertation that nobody else will ever read. Due to Confucius's long-lasting influence, the practice of keeping a cadre of junior scholars to help with research, teaching, and plant watering/cat-sitting duties quickly spread throughout the civilized world (i.e., everywhere except Europe).

---

[6]Interestingly, it was a book written by one of Confucius's contemporaries – *The Art of War* by Sun Tzu – that formalized the practice of MBA students misquoting famous works of literature to justify every unethical business practice they could come up with.

Fig. 6. Confucius Choosing a New Cat Sitter from a List of Desperate Grad Students

The spread of Christianity in Western Europe brought about a transition from cruel, pagan practices (burning people inside a giant wicker man) to modern, civilized behavior (burning people at the stake). The most important of these changes was the creation of monasteries and convents, places where the values that naturally attract grad students – compulsory celibacy, endless study, and artisanal mead making – were strictly enforced. The monks and nuns who lived during the Medieval period lead highly regulated lives: prayers at 2AM, chores at 3AM, and spending 4AM to midnight grading assignments written by local peasants while trying to properly format a bibliography hastily etched on dried goat skin.

**Fig. 7. Medieval Grad Student Using an Early
Version of Microsoft Word**

Despite these challenging circumstances, some Medieval grad students did manage to complete their studies and achieved renown as scholars. One such figure, Francis of Assisi, was so inspired by his life as a grad student that he founded a whole society – the Franciscan Order – based on the principles of poverty, chastity, obedience, and telling everybody you could win on *Jeopardy!* Moreover, St. Francis is often depicted posing with animals, showing his communion with nature, and also how Medieval grad students relied on dog walking as their primary source of income.

Many Medieval scholars, including St. Francis, also experienced *stigmata* – bleeding wounds on their hands and feet – believe to represent either Christ's wounds on the cross or the cheap footwear, carpal tunnel syndrome, and lack of basic hygiene common among grad students in the 13th (and 21st) century. In short, life as a grad student in the Medieval Ages was harsh and difficult, but compared to regular people – i.e., peasants and serfs – life as a grad student was sweet and cushy. We can see here the origin of the idea of grad school as an escape from reality.

Today's grad students have it much worse. They experience all the same drudgery, burnout, low pay, and a surprisingly high number of *stigmata* in the workplace. The difference today is that work outside of academia typically does not involve toiling in a pit of filth all day (unless you work for Elon Musk). In fact, when many modern grad students finish their degrees, they find that life has passed them by and that their friends from undergrad have gone on to buy houses, start families, and stop scavenging for garlic bread from the dumpster behind the Olive Garden.

But this doesn't mean you shouldn't go to grad school. Far from it. But you've got to be prepared. Let this chapter's how to guides and grad student testimonials show you how to do grad school the right way.[7]

How to Finish Your Dissertation Before the Heat Death and Gradual Extinction of the Universe

Writing a dissertation is a huge undertaking! Let this simple, day-by-day guide show you the easiest possible way to get it done on time.

Day 1: Find a desk in the office you share with ten other grad students, set up your computer, and create a new document called "Dissertation.docx." You're really going to do this. Starting tomorrow.

Day 2: Remember *Minesweeper*? You rediscover *Minesweeper*. But you also write the words "When the." Your first two words! Only 69,998 more to go.

Day 3: A small hiccup. A sign on your office door informs you that it is being turned into a private sauna for the university's senior administration. Okay, okay, you can deal with this. You just need to find somewhere else to work.

---

[7]DISCLAIMER: Due to circumstances beyond the author's and the publisher's control, the "right way" still involves a moderate amount of scavenging for garlic bread from the dumpster behind the Olive Garden.

Day 8: After several days testing out cafés, you finally settle on a table at the Wendy's across the street from your apartment. You buy a Frosty and a baked potato to justify staying there for five hours. You don't get any writing done, but you do google "calories in a Frosty" before purchasing two more of them to eat at home in bed.

Day 165: You spend enough time at Wendy's that they offer you a job as an Assistant Manager. You crunch the numbers and realize you will make significantly more than you do as a Teaching Assistant. You accept. You convince yourself that you will be able to work on your dissertation during your breaks. You will also get a discount on Frostys and baked potatoes, which is the only thing you have eaten for the past four months.

Day 751: It's been two years and you've only managed to write ten pages. You also get fired from Wendy's for hiding library books in the walk-in refrigerator. You spot a poster looking for volunteers for a scientific experiment at the university. Desperate for some kind of change in your life, you email the lead scientist.

Day 752: The scientist running the experiment tells you she's working on cryogenic freezing. She wants to freeze you for a month and you'll get $600. It's not much, but it's enough to support you while you make a real push on your first chapter. You sign the waiver and step into the cryogenic chamber.

Day 183,244: Light. Sound. You are suddenly awake, gasping for air. Has it been a month? The screen on the cryogenic chamber says that 500 years have passed. Your dissertation was due 498 years ago. You are trying to calculate how many semesters worth of tuition you owe when a man in a silver suit grabs your arm and pulls you out of the chamber.

Day 183,245: The man in the silver suit explains that the scientist who froze you was denied tenure and quit academia. Everyone at the university forgot about you for centuries, until you were purchased as cargo for an interstellar voyage. He tells you that the next habitable planet is eight light years away. You figure this should give you enough time to finish your first chapter. Or at least most of it.

Day 183,260: You meet the man in the silver suit again. He tells you he is researching the space-time continuum. You try to play *Minesweeper* on one of his computers, but the technology is confusing, and you press the wrong button. Your vision blurs and you feel yourself traveling... somewhere.

Day 27,145,729: You find yourself in a pocket outside of space and time. What feels like mere minutes to you takes countless millennia on the outside. You do not require food, drink, or sleep in this place. You have all the time in the universe. There is nothing but a desk and a computer in front of you. Unfortunately, the computer has *Minesweeper* on it.

Day ???: You have almost finished writing your dissertation (you are also really, really good at *Minesweeper*). Just one more chapter to go. Oh, and a conclusion. Plus, you need to format your bibliography. On the outside, the universe approaches maximum entropy and heat death. There are no more stars, or planets, or dissertation committees. You tell yourself there is still time to add that footnote on Derrida.

Day ∞: The universe collapses into an impossibly dense singularity. Just before the new Big Bang occurs, you add the final word to your dissertation. Every atom of your being is blasted across the vast expanse of space. You are part of the miracle of creation. You also realize that you forgot to save any of the changes you made to your Word document over the last several billion years.

Day 1 (again): You drop out of grad school and get a job at Pizza Hut. That'll show those assholes at Wendy's for firing you.

FAMOUS ADJUNCTS IN HISTORY: No. 3

JESUS OF NAZARETH

Despite a full-time position teaching carpentry at the Nazareth Technical School for Woodworking, Fishing, and Mystical Visions, Jesus decided that he wanted to pursue his passion for theology and began wandering from town-to-town lecturing. Like most modern adjunct professors, Jesus dressed in rags and was not paid for his teaching. Jesus's belief that he was God, however, meant that he had much more in common with today's college presidents. An extremely influential teacher, his Rate My Professor page is chock full of students who hope he will return despite his 2000-year absence.

Jesus holding his office hours outside
(Courtesy Pontius Pilate, VP Faculty Relations)

PROFILES IN FAILURE:
My Name Is Gregor Samsa and This Time I Woke Up as a Grad Student at Cal State San Bernadino

You've probably heard about the first time this happened to me. You know: guy goes to sleep, wakes up as a giant bug, freaks out his family, worries about losing his job, and his dad throws an apple at him. It's a tale as old as time. And, I'm not going to lie, it was a huge pain in the ass. Life as a bug was rough. Eating rotten food and scurrying around all day isn't as fun as it sounds. But the worst part was all the essays college students were forced to write about how what happened to me was supposed to represent man's inhumanity to man or whatever. Give me a fucking break.

What you probably don't know is that life gradually got better for me. Yes, I was still a disgusting bug, but I was able to make the best of things. I built up a pretty big following on TikTok, and before long my sponsored content and merch sales were more than enough to cover my family's monthly expenses. Even my father admitted that I had made something of myself. It wasn't perfect by any means, but for the first time in a long time, I felt like I'd found my place in the world, even if it took a bizarre metamorphosis to bring it about.

And then it happened again. I went to bed on my cozy bug's nest of straw and wood shavings, and I woke up on a third-hand Ikea futon being propped up with a copy of Judith Butler's *Gender Trouble*. I was human again, but just barely. I stumbled out of my bedroom to discover that I shared this tiny, squalid apartment with a person named Thad who claimed to be a part-time barista and a full-time experimental sound artist. Thad offered me a sip from his can of Red Bull and played some of his latest sound art for me. I know I have described many of the indignities I have experienced in life, but listening to Thad's "art" was so traumatic that language alone cannot capture the sense of dread and horror that I felt. Once the horrendous sounds abated, I felt the need to escape from this apartment and never return. Fortunately, Thad told me that I was expected at work.

Apparently, I worked as a teaching assistant somewhere called "Cal State San Bernadino" where I was a graduate student. In my old life, in Prague, scholars were among the most respected people in the city. I was delighted to learn about my new fate; it almost made up for being exposed to Thad's "schizo-rhizomatic soundscape." Naturally, I expected a private limousine with a driver to pull up in front of my apartment building, as was the case with the other doctors and professors that I knew back home. At this point, Thad told me that I would need to take the bus. He showed me the bus pass in my wallet, along with several credit cards that he told me were all maxed out. I felt a pit of dread opening in my stomach, the same feeling I had as a bug when I thought somebody might step on me. The bus pulled up and I got on board.

When I arrived at the campus I was told I would be brought to my office, but this turned out to be just the latest of the lies I have been subjected to. When I pictured a scholar's office, I imagined a grand den, lined with mahogany bookshelves, and filled with ancient tomes and the latest scientific equipment, not unlike Dr. Freud's office at Berggasse 19 in Vienna (I was sent there after the whole "bug thing" happened). What I was shown was an abandoned janitor's closet that had most likely been used as a nest/bathroom/breeding den by a colony of feral cats. There was no window, a single desk, a defunct vending machine, and twenty other grad students who "shared" this space with me. These were the saddest looking people I had ever seen; compared to them, even Thad looked like Archduke Franz Ferdinand or Czar Nicholas.

One of them handed me a stack of paper almost a meter high. They told me that these were my share of the freshman comp essays and that I needed to finish grading them by 5 o'clock. They also said that, even though the papers had students' names on them, almost all of them were actually written by someone called "A.I." I asked why this A.I. was writing all of the students' papers for them, but nobody seemed to know. When I asked them why we allowed this to happen, one of the grad students said we were supposed to "critically embrace generative A.I. technology." When I asked what that meant, nobody had an answer. I sat down to look at the essays.

The ones written by this A.I. person were easy to spot: bland, boring, and full of cliches. The writing was fine, but lifeless, as if it had been created by some kind of automaton like the Golem of Prague (good buddy of mine and a great guy by the way!). One of the TAs told me it was school policy to just give those papers a B- and forget about it, which was easy enough to do. The papers actually written by students were usually more interesting, but also filled with errors. I gave all of them a B- too, except for one which I gave an A+. That one was about me.

This student seemed to have stumbled across that famous short story about my life as a bug. I'd read this story before, of course, but now that I was a grad student instead of a disgusting cockroach, it resonated in a different way for me. The student's description of my strange transformation, my disgusting bug's body, my hideous diet, and my isolation from my family and friends made me feel extremely nostalgic for that magical time in my life. Nobody named Thad made me listen to terrifying experimental music. Nobody forced me to grade essays in an overcrowded, underground prison cell. I found myself fantasizing about returning to my old life, determined to make the most of it this time. I wandered out of my office, caught the bus home, and – after brushing aside Thad's collection of "rare Japanese funk LPs" – I fell asleep on my futon. I disappeared into a dreamless night.

Again I awoke transformed. Gone was my futon, gone was Thad's rare vinyl, gone was Thad himself (I already liked this new life better). This time, my apartment was pretty sweet. For starters, it was less of an apartment and more of a gigantic mansion in the California mountains with a seven-car garage and an infinity pool. I noticed a small bell on my bedside table. Curious, I picked it up and rang it. Instantly a team of servants – some of whom I recognized from the TA office – came rushing in carrying flowers, breakfast, and a Microsoft Excel spreadsheet called "Emergency Financial Contingency Plan – Faculty Cuts." Glancing at the spreadsheet while my underlings stared at me in rapt silence, it suddenly hit me: I was the University President.

Forget the whole bug thing, this new life ruled. All I had to do was hand out honorary doctorates to brain dead tech bros, solicit donations from weapons manufacturers and fossil fuel powerhouses, and rubber stamp plans to raze the library and begin construction on an on-campus lazy river. And if anybody ever questioned any of my decisions, I could fire them! It was a perfect existence. I just had to make sure I never feel asleep. If my life as a travelling salesman got me turned into a bug, this new life was going to get me something much, much worse.

How to Explain to Your Friends and Family that Grad School Definitely Isn't a Cult

Some naysayers will tell you that grad school is a scam or, even worse, a cult. Here's what you can say to shut down the haters!

Talking Point #1: Cults Prey on the Weak and Feeble-Minded by Making Outrageous and Impossible Promises

I mean, sure, I can see what they're implying here, but it's a very superficial comparison. After all, what percentage of those Heaven's Gate weirdos really ended up on a UFO trailing the Hale-Bopp Comet? And how many of *those* people achieved extraterrestrial immortality? Maybe 5%? Well, the number of new grad students who eventually get a tenure-track job is much closer to six – or even seven (!) – percent, so obviously this is an apples-and-oranges situation.

Talking Point #2: Cults Cheat Their Victims Out of Their Life Savings

There's really nothing to talk about here. Cults convince people to turn over their house, assets, and savings account in order to join, whereas people who decide to go to grad school don't have any of that stuff to begin with. Instead, grad school convinces people to take on even more student debt, which means that once they graduate they will need to accept any academic job at all, no matter how poorly paid and demoralizing, and… hmm. Let's move on to the next talking point, shall we?

Talking Point #3: Cults Use Starvation and Sleep Deprivation to Keep Their Victims Weak and Easy to Influence

Shit, okay… next one.

Talking Point #4: Cults Are Structured Around a Single God-Like Personality

My PhD supervisor, Brian, says this isn't true. I know it's a controversial opinion, and yes, I once got into a drunken argument with a table full of sociology grad students while defending Brian's scholarship, but that's just what a good grad student does. Or at least that's what Brian told me. To be honest, Brian has taught me everything I know about academia, work, life, and how to water his house plants when he's out of town for a while. He's my everything. I sleep on a cot on his office floor and make offerings to a small statue of him I've forged out of Play-Doh. So I think I'll let him decide whether I'm in a cult or not!

Talking Point #5: It Can Take Years to Deprogram a Former Cult Member

That sounds horrific. I'm glad I've avoided anything like that by spending the past twelve years writing a dissertation about how great Brian is.

ACADEMIC GLOSSARY

GRE: A standardized test to evaluate your aptitude for grad school. The GRE tests the "big three" values any grad student needs: Grit, Resilience, and Eating Garlic Bread from the Dumpster Behind Olive Garden.

Teaching Assistant: Many grad students are also offered a job as a "Teaching Assistant" or "TA." TAs assist professors by leading tutorials, grading student work, and explaining the professor's outdated cultural references to a room full of baffled eighteen-year-olds.

Funding Package: In order to fund the university, grad students are expected to deliver a package to their supervisor – also known as an "underboss" or "*capo*" – once a week. Where they get the money is up to them, but the most common sources are TA work, part-time serving jobs, and protection rackets run out of the library's rare books room. For late payments, the vig is four points per week. For really late payments, the penalty is death or working as an adjunct professor, depending on current staffing needs and/or connections in the old country (Harvard).

Dissertation Committee: A panel of professors who will decide whether your dissertation is up to snuff. Typically comprised of one professor from each of the university's "four families": Arts, Sciences, Humanities, and the Gambino crime syndicate (typically housed within business schools). The committee can declare a dissertation a pass (with honors), a pass, a pass with revisions, a fail, or the dreaded *Il baccio della disoccupazione* ("kiss of unemployment").

PhD: You know this one, lol. PRETTY. HUGE. DEBT TOLLERANCE THRESHOLD.

Quiz: Academic You Cite in Your Dissertation or Character from James Clavell's *Shogun*?

1) Vasco Rodrigues
2) Sianne Ngai
3) Andreas Malm
4) Martin Alvito
5) Giorgio Agamben
6) Toda Mariko
7) Bruno Latour
8) Hendrik Specz
9) Peter Stallybrass
10) Alban Caradoc
11) Johann Vinck
12) Peter Sloterdijk
13) Carlo Dell'Acqua
14) Antonio Negri
15) Franco Moretti
16) Nebara Jozen
17) Lauren Berlant
18) Paulus Spillbergen
19) Slavoj Žižek
20) John Blackthorne

Academic You Cite in Your Dissertation: 2, 3, 5, 7, 9, 12, 14, 15, 17, 19
Character from James Clavell's *Shogun*: 1, 4, 6, 8, 10, 11, 13, 16, 18, 20

Fig. 8. Behind the Numbers: Graduate Student Housing

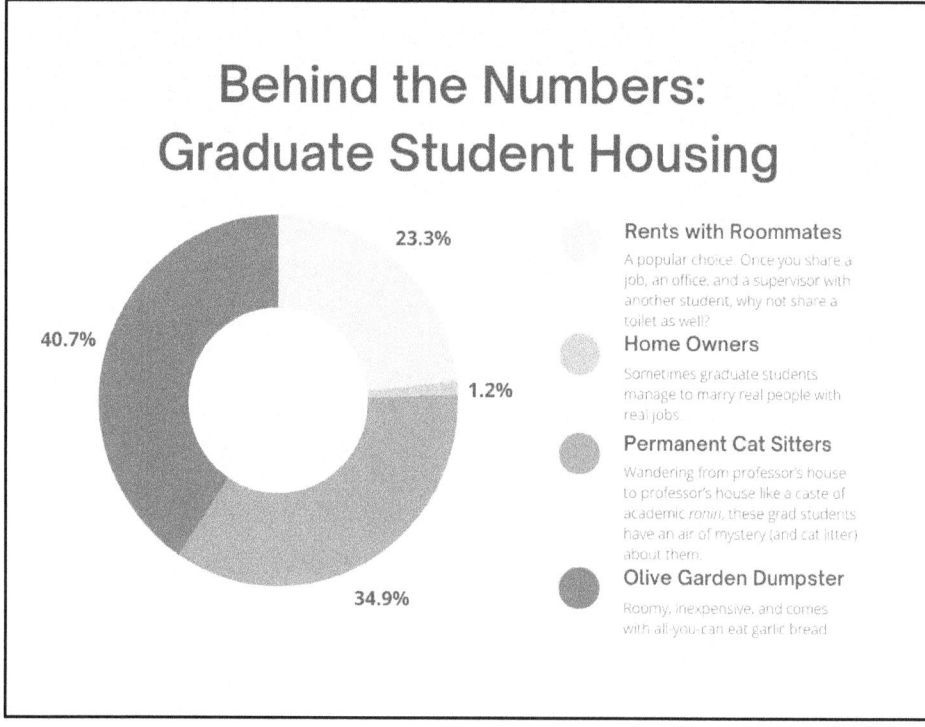

CHAPTER III:
The Job Market

So you finished your PhD! Maybe it took five years, maybe it took ten, maybe you didn't finish yet and you're cheating by reading ahead. That's okay, I forgive you.[8] At some point toward the end of your time in grad school, your thoughts probably drifted toward the academic job market. The term "job market" can be a little deceptive, though. To be clear, it really is a market, where you will be examined, poked, and prodded like an underripe plum at Trader Joe's. The word "job," however, implies that jobs in academia actually exist, which they don't, at least not on a full-time, well-paid basis. But the whole "job market" thing is a fun game academics like to play with each other, so if you're going to squat in the Ivory Tower for a while, you'd better learn how to play along.

As always, *How to Succeed in Academia* has got you covered. This chapter will teach you everything you need to know about pretending you are trying to get a job that hasn't existed since 1985. You will also learn a little bit about ancient demons and necromancy, both of which – unlike the job market – are quite serious and real.

The academic job market as we know it today emerged during what academics call the Early Modern Period, or what normal people call the Renaissance. It was a time of creative explosion in literature, music, and the arts, and so of course the people who did those things needed a side hustle to pay the bills. For many, academia seemed like the perfect solution, especially compared to earlier side hustles like backbreaking farm labor and leper washing. The tricky part was getting a foot in the door, in most cases quite literally, as convents and monasteries were

---

[8]DISCLAIMER: The author's forgiveness requires a $50 administrative fee each time you disappoint him. Expect an invoice once you finish this book.

unwilling to open up and let in thousands of decadent newcomers (they were already at capacity). But the Renaissance also saw a massive increase in the number of new universities, including schools like Oxford, the Sorbonne, and the University of Phoenix Online.[9]

Of course, even this glut of new universities couldn't provide as many jobs as there were job seekers, so an early version of the job market gradually emerged. Although the term "job market" has been around since Biblical times (see below), the first modern academic job market emerged in Florence, Italy in the fifteenth century. One family – the Medici – dominated banking, politics, textile trading, and beer pong during this period, and so they naturally decided to branch out into higher education.

Fig. 9. Cosimo de Medici Offering a Four-Month Contract to an Adjunct Professor

Many of the most famous artists of Renaissance Italy had received money from the Medici for their art, so it was understandable that quite a few of them also tried to get paid for teaching classes in sculpture, painting, and Writing for Business Students 101. The head of the House of Medici – and VP of Faculty Relations – Cosimo de' Medici quickly

---

[9]In this context, "Phoenix" referred to the mythical bird, not the city in Arizona. And "online" simply meant that all classes were conducted while students were strung up on a line being beaten for minor offenses like blasphemy or urinating on one of the King's swans.

noticed a problem of supply and demand. If you needed someone to carve a giant marble statue of David, there was really only one guy for the job, and so you needed to pay him. But if you needed someone to teach, say, three sections of "Intro to Art History," you could hire pretty much anybody, so why not make the hiring process as needlessly complicated and soul-crushing as possible?

FAMOUS ADJUNCTS IN HISTORY: No. 8

WILLIAM SHAKESPEARE

As the eldest son of a successful glove maker, Shakespeare had connections in the world of higher education, provided he was willing to teach courses in glove history and glove appreciation. Sadly, Shakespeare shrugged off the benefits of nepotism, and decided to go his own way and bring shame upon his family by writing disreputable comedies and plays about weird guys who talk to skulls. This did not pay the bills, so he had to resort to teaching creative writing and improv workshops most evenings. He died while soliciting audience suggestions for "a body part that starts with the letter P."

Courtesy King's Men Dramatic Academy Website

A standard academic job interview under the House of Medici involved a teaching demo, a meeting with the hiring committee, and an attempted poisoning. Candidates who survived the poisoning would move on to the next round. Candidates who failed at either the teaching demo or the meeting would be poisoned.[10] Eventually, the surviving candidates were so grateful to have had their teaching and scholarship recognized (and to not have been poisoned) that they accepted whatever salary they were offered.

Has the job market changed much in the past 500 years? Yes. While there are fewer poisonings, there are also fewer jobs. Does that

---

[10]This model of constantly poisoning (and re-poisoning) job seekers remained standard practice at most European universities until the 1970s and the publication of Michel Foucault's influential volume *Discipline and Poison: The Birth of the University and the Death – by Poison – of Most of My Friends* (Gallimard, 1975).

mean all hope is lost and you'll never get an academic job? Yes. But look, I want you to finish reading my book, so let's pretend for now that you actually have a shot at getting a tenure-track job and that something I'm going to say might help you. So read on, job seeker! I know you can do it![11]

Academic Job Ads: What They Say Vs. What They Mean

Academic job ads can be confusing! Let this guide show you how to read between the lines and figure out what job ads are really saying.

What they say: 2/2 teaching load.
What they mean: It will actually be a 4/4 after two years of budget cuts and faculty attrition.

What they say: Some service work is involved.
What they mean: You will spend every evening and weekend answering emails and attending Zoom meetings.

What they say: We welcome all applicants.
What they mean: If you already work here as an adjunct professor, don't even think about applying.

What they say: A Ph.D. in a relevant discipline is mandatory.
What they mean: We're sorry, but if you are one of our adjuncts and you're reading this job ad, can we respectfully ask that you log the fuck off? You're not allowed to use campus Wi-Fi, and we don't pay you enough to afford it at home, so unless you're in your faculty office (i.e., Starbucks), we really don't know how the fuck you're even seeing this.

---

[11]DISCLAIMER: The author and publisher legally define "it" as "purchase another copy of this book." All other interpretations are null and void.

Log off, asshole. Don't you have three hundred essays on *As I Lay Dying* or some shit to start grading?

What they say: An excellent record of teaching and supervision.
What they mean: Wait, aren't you that guy Steve or whatever who teaches that god-awful "Folk and Fairy Tales" class that none of the tenured faculty will touch with a ten-foot pole? Get the fuck back to work, Steve! You're wasting your time, and since we're paying you $1,400 this semester, your time is actually our time, motherfucker. Yeah, yeah, you've got a dossier full of letters from students saying how great you are. Here's what you should do with them, Steve-o: Print them out, put them in a huge fucking pile, and take a big old dump right on top of them. That's all they're good for, Steve! Wipe your ass with a few of them for all we give a shit. Then set the whole thing on fire. Fuck off.

What they say: Peer-reviewed publications and a five-year research plan are required.
What they mean: You've got to be fucking kidding me, Steve. If you think anybody in the world gives half a flying fuck about your "forthcoming" (fuck you!) essay on Hans Christian Andersen and the "folkloric tradition" (whatever the fuck that means!), you're even fucking stupider than we thought, and we already thought you were a pure fucking moron. Look, Steve, we're going to level with you: once you agree to start working here as an adjunct, we own your fucking soul. That's not a metaphor, either—it's in your contract. What's that, Steve? You didn't read all the fine print? Tough shit, asshole. We're sick of dealing with your bullshit, so we're turning you over to our VP of Human Resources, Mephistopheles. Technically he's the one who owns your soul, so try bitching to him for a change and see how far that gets you, you fucking dipshit.

What they say: Come join our diverse and inclusive department.
What they mean: STEVE, THIS IS THE DEMON MEPHISTOPHELES
I AM COMING FOR YOUR SOUL TONIGHT AT MIDNIGHT,
STEVE. BE AFRAID, STEVE, BE VERY, VERY AFRAID!

What they say: Tenure-track.
What they mean: This job search will be canceled. Oh, and we're
looking for someone to replace Steve. Nobody has seen that fucking guy
for the past three weeks.

Fig. 10. Behind the Numbers: Academic Job Ads

Behind the Numbers: Academic Job Ads

23.3%

40.7%

1.2%

34.9%

Police Sting Operations
Fake job ads designed to catch
adjuncts who owe thousands in
unpaid bus fare.

Genuine Job Postings
All of these job searches were
eventually cancelled.

Little Caesars
An effective, if deceptive, way for the
pizza chain to find workers with low
salary expectations.

Cat Sitters
Tenured professors need cat sitters
and this is the easiest way to find
someone who has no money and
can use a can opener.

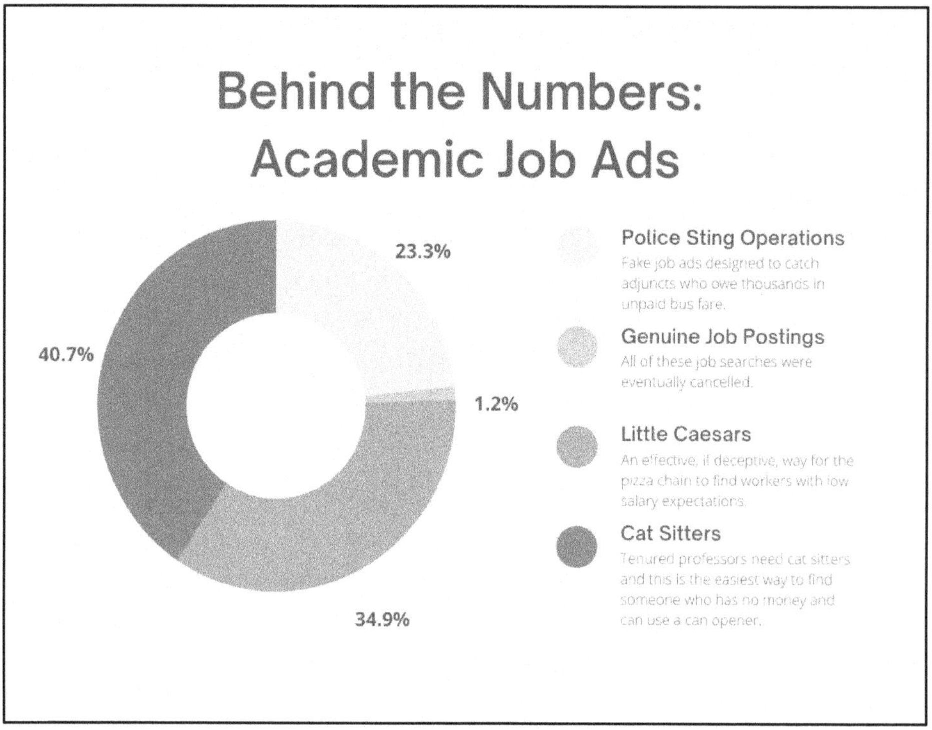

How to Apply for an Academic Job and Summon the Ancient Mesopotamian Demon Pazuzu

Applying for an academic job is a huge undertaking! With a bit of help from us (and also from a primordial evil entity) you will get your application submitted in no time at all.

Step One: The Job Search

Keep an eye out for job postings in the usual places: the *Chronicle of Higher Education*, faculty listservs, and esoteric manuscripts hidden in the Vatican library. Pay particular attention to jobs located near the Tigris and Euphrates rivers in the Fertile Crescent region. Job ads written in Sumerian cuneiform should go in the "definitely apply" pile. Same goes for any job that offers to pay you in livestock, grain, or small golden trinkets. If you're not sure if a job is right for you, try staring into a broken mirror and saying the name of the school 666 times. If the mirror starts to bleed, you're definitely on the right track.

Step Two: Formatting Your C.V.

Some basics:
- 8.5"x11" paper
- 1" margins
- single-spaced
- 12-point font (ideally Sumerian cuneiform)
- outline major scholastic achievements, in reverse chronological order, recorded in the blood of a newly slaughtered ram
- place the finished document in an envelope, and then place the envelope in a 3,000-year-old Babylonian urn, which you should bury under the search committee chair's office
- be sure to include graduate transcripts, an academic writing sample, and a mummified goat fetus to make your application really stand out

Fig. 11. Noted Academic Job Search Advice Guru/Ancient Demon Pazuzu

Step Three: The Cover Letter

List all of the worldly goods (grain reserves, coin hoards, first-born children) you would be willing to sacrifice to get this job. Two pages, single-spaced, maximum. Address the letter "To whom it may concern," throw it into the Dead Sea, and get ready to play the waiting game.

Step Four: The Waiting Game

Wake up every morning and check the Academic Jobs Wiki. Then check to see if your bathtub is filled with blood. If it is, congratulations! This means the Mesopotamian demon Pazuzu has accepted your offer. Using the Babylonian urn you buried under the chair's office as a portal from the netherworld to this plane of existence, he has infiltrated the campus and possessed the search committee chair. Later that day, you will watch seven crows fall from the sky and land in a perfect circle, which signifies that you have been offered a job interview (you will also receive an email about this). Okay, it's time to get excited! Pack your bags! (With a large crucifix and several copper daggers!)

Step Five: The Interview

Sit down with the search committee. Remember: they're nervous too. The search chair seems especially distressed — head rotating 360°, vomiting bile, cursing in an unknown dialect. This could be the result of either demonic possession or a rejected sabbatical application. You need to be sure. Show the chair the large crucifix and copper daggers you brought with you. If he takes one of the daggers and carves the words "Publish or Perish" into his torso, you'll know that Pazuzu is going to force the rest of the committee to hire you. If he tries to stab you with the dagger, he may need more persuading. Try brandishing the crucifix and yelling, "The power of Christ compels you!" (NOTE: If it's a secular school, try yelling something about the power of innovation instead). At this point, Pazuzu will either help you get the job or disappear forever in a cloud of sulfurous black smoke. Regardless, you should thank the committee for their time, go home, and wait for the job offer/writ of ex-communication to arrive in your inbox.

Step Six: Getting Tenure

You'll have five years to publish a book, a dozen journal articles, teach four classes per semester, and sit on an endless procession of committees, all while trying to pay off your student loans and maintain the illusion of a personal life. Sorry, but even an ancient demon like Pazuzu has limits to his powers. We suggest seeking out a truly malevolent source of evil instead, like Baphomet, Beelzebub, or — if things get really desperate — the university president's office.

PROFILES IN FAILURE:
I'm Job from the Bible and the Academic Job Market Is Named After Me

I thought God and I were cool. I had a nice little life: a sweet farm in the Land of Uz, lots of kids, and a hot wife. Living the dream, all thanks to the big guy in the sky. I got the feeling that my buddies Eliphaz, Bildad, and Zophar were jealous, but I took care of them too, so they kept quiet about it. Each day was better than the last. Agriculture had just been invented last year, so I was on the cutting edge of the marketplace. Selling grain for two silver coins per bushel? You know I was rolling in it.

And then it all went to shit. I woke up one day covered in itchy boils that were leaking pus. I looked over at the other side of the bed and my beautiful wife has been replaced with a stinky old leper. He said his name was Andy, he was sorry about this, but God and the Devil had made a bet about how much shit they could put me through, and he was part of the plan. I was glad Andy told me what was going on, even if he was kind of decomposing on my best silk sheets. He wasn't such a bad guy, I thought. I wanted to shake his hand or maybe even hug him, but I was worried about catching leprosy on top of the boils. No need to make things worse.

Turns out things couldn't really get any worse. I looked out the window and all my crops had been eaten by a plague of locusts. The sun was baking the earth and all the water from my stream had dried up. All my livestock had keeled over and were being picked apart by vultures. I was ruined. I went to tell my kids that we would need to move to a new farm, but I quickly discovered that they were all dead too. I was leaning over my dead children, bitter tears falling from my eyes, when I felt Andy's strong hand on my shoulder. He was offering to make pancakes.

Sure, I said, that sounds nice. I knew better than to eat food prepared by a leper, but by that point I had stopped caring. My life was already over.

We couldn't make pancakes because I didn't have any grain or water and also because my hearth had been destroyed by an earthquake. We decided to eat chips of dried mud instead. I was munching on my second mud chip when Eliphaz, Bildad, and Zophar pulled up on their mules.

"This place looks like shit," Bildad said.

"We heard God was playing a prank on you," Zophar said.

I asked them about this prank, and they said it was pretty simple. The Devil bet that if God took everything away from me, I would despair and curse God's name. For some reason, God took this bet, and yeah, you've already seen what happened next. But I refused to turn away from God. As bad as this was, God had only taken away what he gave me in the first place. It might not be fair, but it didn't mean God was any less powerful. My friends just shook their heads and rode away.

Andy was whipping up another batch of mud cakes when the sky darkened and lightning crashed all around us. It seemed that God and the Devil had heard what I said and decided to raise the stakes. There was a great flash of light that blinded my eyes. When my vision returned, I was in a place that was completely strange to me. I was no longer naked but dressed in a suit made of cheap fabric that did not fit properly. I was seated on an uncomfortable chair in a hallway just outside a room with numbers on the door. Andy was nowhere to be seen.

I looked around and noticed that I wasn't the only one waiting in this hallway. In front of most of the numbered doors there was a sad and terrified-looking person perched on a chair. I approached one of these pathetic creatures and asked a few questions. His name was Dennis, and he was here for a "job interview." I asked some follow-up questions. Even though they were pretty weird questions, Dennis didn't seem bothered at all. It was like he'd come here prepared to answer whatever ridiculous inquiry came his way. He told me the year was 2012 and we were in a foreign city-state named "Seattle." The purpose of this gathering was something called "the MLA convention." Just as I was about to ask what that meant, the door beside Dennis creaked open and somebody called his name. He looked at me the way a goat does before you slit its throat. I walked back to my chair and waited my turn. I could tell that whatever happened next would be God's harshest and most severe test yet of my resolve.

Moments later the door creaked open and a voice beckoned me inside. I stood up and entered, muttering a tiny prayer as I did so. I felt like I was entering the den of Satan himself. I was led into a large room, where I was told to sit on a bed. Surrounding the bed, sitting in armchairs, were some of the strangest people I had ever seen in my life. They had gaudy jewelry, dated suits, and what I could only assume were self-inflicted haircuts. One of them wore a t-shirt promoting something called "Buffy the Vampire Slayer." It was only once this ordeal was over that I would learn these creatures are known as "tenured professors."

And then the questions began. Not normal questions like, "how many silver coins for this bushel of grain?", but bizarre, unanswerable questions about how I might teach a class I had never heard of, or what I might want to write about five years from now. Eventually, they started bickering with each other. The man with the "Buffy the Vampire Slayer" t-shirt accused a woman with chunky green earrings of "sabotaging" the search because she "just wanted to hire another Medievalist," while chunky earrings then accused the man of not knowing what he was talking about because his PhD was from somewhere called "Dartmouth." Before long they were all yelling at each other and calling each other names. Eventually I slid onto the floor and crawled out of the room on my belly. I don't think any of them noticed.

Once I was back in the hallway, I noticed something in my pocket. I pulled it out. It appeared to be some kind of schedule. If I was interpreting the markings correctly, this interview was only the first of ten I was supposed to attend this week. I saw Dennis back in the hallway, showed him my schedule, and asked if this could be true. All he said was that he was jealous I had so many interviews lined up. I didn't see it that way at all. I saw this for what it was: God's latest, and cruelest, test of my faith.

Thus began the most trying week of my life. After the fifth pointless interview, I contemplated hurling myself from one of the hotel windows (they were locked, no doubt to prevent other cursed souls from ending things this way). By the time my eighth interview was over, I was ready to despair and curse God's name, like my friends had encouraged me to do back at my house. But then I remembered sweet, leprous Andy's advice: the Devil wanted to see if I would break, but if I didn't, God would surely reward me. So I swallowed my pride, entered the next hotel room, and pretended to know what a "learning outcome" was. It was horrible, of course, countless times more horrible than what I had endured in my old life, but eventually it was over.

After my tenth interview, I stumbled out of the hotel room and collapsed in the hallway. I was haunted by dreams about what had transpired in the past week. When I awoke, I was back home, in my bed. Andy was not there, but my wife was, as were all my children. A miracle! I asked if they had seen a really cool and sexy guy who also happened to be a leper, but they hadn't. Bummer. But then I looked out my window, and there he was, feeding my livestock, watering my crops, and seemingly cured of his leprosy. Truly I had been restored to my riches, but with Andy in the mix I felt twice as wealthy as I was before. I ran outside to give him a hug, ignoring the cries and complaints of my wife and children.

I was then that God spoke to me. He said he was pleased to see the strength of my faith, that I never despaired, and that's why he restored my worldly success. I started babbling about how much I appreciated the Andy thing, but God cut me off before I could really get started. He told me that to commemorate my piety, he would name the horrible ordeal I endured in the hotel after me. He would use this horrific ritual to torture those who displeased him for the rest of eternity. I said I was cool with that, and then I asked God if he could maybe give me and Andy some time to ourselves. At that point he sighed and disappeared in a puff of smoke. Fair enough, I guess. But it pleased me to know that the "Job market" would live on well beyond my natural life. Maybe not the nicest legacy, but hey, you've got to have something.

At some point people stopped pronouncing it "Jobe" and started saying "Jawb," like a bunch of idiots. Andy told me to complain to God about it, but he stopped taking my calls centuries ago. No biggie. Besides,

I've got bigger things to worry about. Andy and I are trying to find just the right resort for our vacation on the bank of the Euphrates, and I'm constantly trying to dodge that lawyer my ex-wife and kids hired to shake me down. Sometimes it's stressful, but whenever I feel like despairing, I just remember my time in the cursed Land of Seattle, and all my stress dissolves. When you've already been through hell, everything else seems like heaven.

ACADEMIC GLOSSARY

Search Committee: If you want a tenure-track job, you're going to need a whole committee to help you search for one. Looking for jobs posted online is just the tip of the iceberg. You're going to need to print "Professor for Hire" posters to tape to lamp posts and laundromat bulletin boards. You're going to need a squad of secret agents (known as "honeypots") to seduce and blackmail senior academic administrators. And you're going to need your parents to tell you to just walk into the local university and ask if they need anybody (little known fact: this is how 90% of all Baby Boomers received their tenure-track jobs).

LTA: Stands for limited-term Assistant Professor. Inspired by the hit 1994 film *Speed*, in which a city bus will detonate if it travels slower than 50 miles per hour, many schools now hire Assistant Professors whose term will be limited (i.e., they will be fired) if they grade fewer than 50 assignments per day. Most firings are accompanied by a pre-recorded video featuring *Speed* star Dennis Hopper, though confusingly he appears as his character Frank Booth from the 1984 film *Blue Velvet*. Most LTAs describe it as "the most disturbing thing they have ever seen."

First-Round Interview: A typical academic interview will involve a committee asking questions to a candidate who is trying to survive a 3-minute round in the ring with former Heavyweight champion "Iron" Mike Tyson. Those who survive the 3-minutes and satisfactorily answer the committee's questions, will collaborate with Tyson on a teaching demonstration.

Quiz: Should I Work as an Adjunct Professor?

Question 1: What is your favorite meal?
   a) Risotto with freshly shaved white truffles eaten in Emilia-Romagna
   b) T-bone Wagyu steak eaten in Lower Manhattan
   c) Fresh otoro and uni sashimi eaten in Tokyo
   d) Four-day old Subway Cold Cut Trio eaten over the kitchen sink

Question 2: What are you most looking for in a romantic partner?
   a) Physical attraction
   b) Compatible personality
   c) Sense of humor
   d) Netflix password and/or non-expired credit card

Question 3: What is your dream home?
   a) Downtown penthouse with private swimming pool
   b) Country estate with 20-acre garden
   c) Just, like, a normal house somewhere
   d) Basement apartment you share with a sociopath named Craig and several million cockroaches

Question 4: How often should you receive a raise at work?
   a) Whenever you ask for one
   b) Every six months
   c) Every year

d) Hahahahahahahahahahahahahahahahahahasobsobsobsobsobsobsobs obsob

Question 5: What do you most value in your coworkers?
a) Teamwork and collaboration
b) Communication and transparency
c) Hard work and dedication
d) No longer stealing your Oreos after you threatened them with a rusty switchblade

ANSWER KEY: D, of course, but let's be honest: if you're wondering if you should work as an adjunct professor, it means you're out of options. It's happening, motherfucker. Turn to the next chapter and start praying for a tenured professor with good insurance to hit you with their car.

CHAPTER IV:
Working as an Adjunct Professor

Your first year on the job market was a success, provided you define "success" as "I wasn't gunned down by an on-campus shooter during one of my job interviews."[12] By pretty much any other definition of success, you fucking failed. Not that it's your fault! Well, it's kind of your fault for not listening to all those people (your parents, your friends, the Pope, probably, if you'd bothered to ask him) who told you not to go to grad school in the first place. But the system *was* rigged against you and 99.9% of all the other people who applied for a tenure-track job last year. There is a kind of consolation prize, though. You will still get to teach a class at a university, and you will even get to call yourself a professor! The only catch is that you will have to subsist on the same diet and salary as a Norwegian fish cleaner from 1905 (not adjusted for inflation). Now if an endless supply of fish heads and four bronze *kroner* per month doesn't sound that bad to you (and after ten years of grad school, it probably doesn't), read on and learn about the other benefits of working in the glamorous field of adjunct professorhood. But before we get down to real world, practical advice (like what to do if you're six raccoons in an upscale winter jacket or what might happen if you drink from the wrong holy grail), let's take a look at the history of the adjunct professor, from ancient times to the present day. Much of this research required painstaking hours searching through archives, but since we made adjunct professors do it, we don't have to pay them for any of it. The system works (unless you're an adjunct)!

---

[12]If this did happen to you, a) we're sorry, and b) can you please let us know how many copies of this book we're selling in the afterlife? We will need those numbers if *How to Succeed in Academia* is going to get optioned as an Apple TV+ Original (starring Gary Oldman as the ancient Mesopotamian demon "Pazuzu").

The

True & Surprizing

NATURAL HISTORY
of
The Adjunct Professor;
being an account of the poverty, suffering
degradation, grading, &c., &c., &c.,
of these most miserable of creatures

As related by the wise and underpaid
DOCTOR BULLEN

Published by the disreputable rogues at
Humorist Books
of *NEW YORK CITY*

PART ONE: THE FOSSIL RECORD

Paleontologists agree on three fundamental facts about our earliest ancestors: they lived in small social groups, they used tools for hunting and skinning animals, and they offloaded most of their teaching and grading to an underclass of individuals who were excluded from mainstream society (a.k.a., the first adjunct professors). The fossil record suggests that these early adjuncts were undernourished, unhappy, and overworked (most died on top of a pile of unfinished lesson plans). The social cost of being an early adjunct professor was considerable. These creatures were required to sleep at least 50 feet away from the communal fire, and – based on fossilized hip bones and pornographic cave drawings – were exceedingly unpopular as sexual partners.

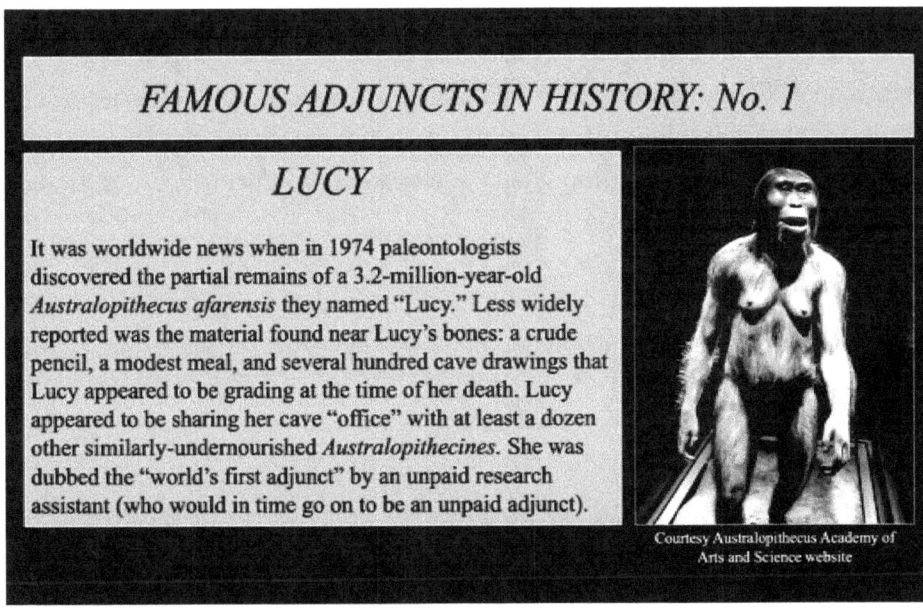

FAMOUS ADJUNCTS IN HISTORY: No. 1

LUCY

It was worldwide news when in 1974 paleontologists discovered the partial remains of a 3.2-million-year-old *Australopithecus afarensis* they named "Lucy." Less widely reported was the material found near Lucy's bones: a crude pencil, a modest meal, and several hundred cave drawings that Lucy appeared to be grading at the time of her death. Lucy appeared to be sharing her cave "office" with at least a dozen other similarly-undernourished *Australopithecines*. She was dubbed the "world's first adjunct" by an unpaid research assistant (who would in time go on to be an unpaid adjunct).

Courtesy Australopithecus Academy of Arts and Science website

As early humans began to leave Africa and spread throughout Europe and Asia, the traditions associated with adjunct professors began to change, though their lowly place in society remained a universal constant. The Neanderthals, for example, were the first group of humans to trick adjuncts into teaching for even longer by dangling the promise of a more permanent position (such as Lecturer, Assistant Professor, or

Bone Enchantress) in front of them. This strategy allowed the Neanderthals to continue exploiting adjunct professors until as recently as 40,000 years ago, when climate change, competition from Homo sapiens, and faculty-wide budget cuts drove them to extinction.

Early Homo sapiens relied on the cheap labor of adjunct professors, of course, though they also introduced a crucial innovation. By not paying their adjuncts any more than three polished seashells per month, early humans made sure that adjuncts would need a second, third, and fourth source of income. And thus, the side hustle was born. This was one of the most important inventions in human history. Deployed not only on adjuncts but also against artists, musicians, writers, or anyone else who decided to "do what they love," the side hustle is time-honored technique for punishing people who care about things other than money. According to paleontologists, the most common side hustles among early Homo sapiens were babysitting, food preparation, and driving for Uber.[13] For most primitive adjuncts, these side hustles eventually became their permanent form of employment, as most of their teaching and grading duties were eventually outsourced to other, now extinct branches of the human family tree, including *Homo erectus*, *Homo floresiensis*, and even the lowly *Homo adjunctiensis*.

---

[13] Of course, Uber as we think of it today did not exist thousands of years ago when there were no cars, bicycles, or wheels. But Uber has paid the author and publisher a substantial premium (thanks guys!) to pretend that they invented the concepts of ride sharing and getting a cold $40 burrito delivered to your house at 3AM, so that's what we're going with. So, if 80,000 years ago you gave someone a piggyback ride home after a long night out drinking fermented plum juice, congratulations, you drive for Uber now.

The Fossilized Skull of *Homo adjunctiensis*

1) Multiple dents on the skull indicate a habit of banging the head against a hard surface, likely a rock or a desk, possibly due to frustration about the job market.
2) Sloping forehead and thick brow protect against sunlight, to which *Homo adjunctiensis* was rarely exposed due to long working hours and dwelling in "basement" level of caves.
3) Large nose for smelling free food from a considerable distance and for snorting botanical stimulants to stay awake during morning classes.
4) Considerable tooth decay suggests a poor diet, high in naturally occurring sugar and caffeine. Jaw wear suggests grinding due to stress (plus sugar, caffeine, and multiple daily bumps of botanical stimulants).

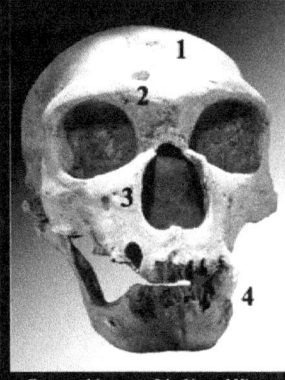

Courtesy Museum of the Natural History of the Adjunct Professor

PART TWO: THE ANCIENT WORLD

It is often said that Rome wasn't built in a day. What gets left out of that expression is that, yes, it took a long time to build ancient monuments like the Colosseum, the Great Pyramids, and Stonehenge, but in financial terms it may as well have only been a day or two, since the adjunct professors who did all the planning, laboring, and most of the catering, were working for free. The dawn of civilization and the invention of agriculture, cities, and animal husbandry was also accompanied by the invention of things like paying your dues, working through the weekend, and napping in the hallway between classes. When adjunct professors failed to thrive at growing wheat or convincing two cows to have sex with each other, they naturally gravitated toward less lucrative career paths. While this involved teaching for very little money, of course, it also involved part-time temple building, mumification, and Druid-assisting duties.

Fig. 12. Adjunct Professors Sharing an Office in Ancient Britain

The Ancient World produced many epic tales describing the adventures and exploits of adjunct professors. The Mesopotamian *Epic of Gilgamesh*, for example, tells the story of a mighty king, who battles and later befriends an unkempt wild man (easily identified as an adjunct professor), before working together to fight the giant Humbaba, slay the Bull of Heaven, and redesign the entire Humanities curriculum while slashing 75% of the faculty budget. In revenge, the Gods kill the wild man due to his lack of health insurance, but are forced to spare the king thanks to his noble spirit and the fact that he has tenure.

Perhaps the most famous ancient epic about an adjunct professor is *The Odyssey*. Credited to Homer, but almost certainly written by a hiring committee, *The Odyssey* details Odysseus' twenty-year voyage home (without departmental funding) after interviewing for a job at the MLA Convention in Troy. During his lengthy, uh, odyssey, Odysseus needs to slay the cyclops Polyphemus, resist the lure of the sirens' song, and work a series of low-paying Research Assistant gigs to save up enough cash for a deposit on an apartment in Ithaca. When he finally arrives home his family does not recognize him, which is a common phenomenon even today when adjuncts return from first-round job interviews. Just as Odysseus settles into his new studio apartment, he receives a letter telling him that he did not get the job he interviewed for. To honor Odysseus, today's academic hiring committees still take twenty years to email unsuccessful job candidates.

PART THREE: ANCIENT GREECE AND ROME, THE MIDDLE AGES, THE RENAISSANCE

Shame on you if you forgot, but we already covered these time periods in earlier chapters. So you could flip back and read them now, like a loser, or you could buy three more copies of this book, cut out the relevant sections, and paste them in on the dotted lines below. I guess it's up to you to decide if you want to be cool about this or not.

--- INSERT ANCIENT GREECE AND ROME SECTION HERE ---

--- INSERT MIDDLE AGES SECTION HERE ---

--- INSERT STATEMENT OF TEACHING PHILOSOPHY HERE (MANDATORY) ---

PART FOUR: PURITANS AND PILGRIMS

When the Pilgrims left England for Holland, and then – finding Holland insufficiently repressive – decided to leave Holland for America, they boarded a Dutch cargo *fluyt* that they called the *Mayflower*. On board were 102 passengers, 30 crew members, and – on the lowest deck of the vessel – 99 adjunct professors. Here are their names:

1. Learnwell Nomoney
2. Laborius Cheaply
3. Regretful Hopkins
4. Studious Smoot
5. Increase Workhours
6. Grading Standish
7. Praise-Innovation Barebone
8. Anger Allerton
9. Longhours Hynde
10. Humiliation Jones
11. Workmuch Billington
12. Sadness Stevens
13. No-tenure Thomas
14. Desk-nap Deakins
15. Constantius Freelunch
16. Futon Browne
17. William Workless
18. Fear-interview Ingersoll
19. Job-talk Firebrand
20. More-teaching Thompson
21. Nathaniel Nojobbe
22. Servius Softmind
23. God-hates-me Harris
24. Lament Lewis

25. Poor-choices Peterson

26. Thomas Tenurefree

27. Works-for-Satan Sunderland

28. Hopeless Prospect

29. Verity Sadsoul

30. Poor-performance Workman

31. Helpless Applicant

32. Sarah Sidehustle

33. Why-me Jones

34. Why-not-me Eaton

35. Anne Slowlearner

36. [Unknown – fired and thrown overboard]

37. [Unknown – fired and thrown overboard]

38. [Unknown – fired and thrown overboard]

39. [Unknown – fired and thrown overboard]

40. Much-mail Inbox

41. Knowledge Freeman

42. Steal-lunch Jenkins

43. Save-me Hoolihan

44. No-references Gardiner

45. James Jobless III

46. Not-by-choice Chastity

47. Rend-pants Robinson

48. Empty Anderson

49. Foolish Phillips

50. Too-busy Burtis

51. Francis Sleepless

52. Solomon Bachelor

53. Justice Jobmarket

54. Praise-labor Suckling

55. Dreary Dennison

56. No-honor Wilson

57. Has-hypertension Cooper

58. Advil Smythe

59. Sleep-all-day Lewis

60. Working More
61. Skin-crawl Cellardweller
62. Gabriel Goutfoot
63. Twelve-ales Everynight
64. Some-scurvy Stevenson
65. Lemuel Littlehope
66. John Coffeecup
67. No-grace Greene
68. Surrender Thomas
69. Come-what-will Crumpler
70. Feckless Finemore
71. Scourge-of-God Sinclair
72. Choose-me Mullins
73. One-shirt O'Neill
74. Thomas Loveless
75. Geoffrey Foulpants
76. Touch-her-parts Patterson
77. Overly Learned
78. Xerox Coverletter
79. Please-no-more Parker
80. Redundant Robertson
81. Some-shame Merrymount
82. Many-books Morton
83. Maximum Drudgery
84. Four-cats Feeney
85. Too-bad Boyle
86. Curriculum Vitae
87. Try-hard Harrison
88. God-knows-why Williams
89. Goodman Grader
90. Frequent Weeping
91. Just-quit-now Norris
92. Internal Candidate
93. Need-hope Hollinghurst
94. Sleeps-alone Busyhands

95. Friendless Fullerton
96. Constant Illness
97. God-regrets-me Miller
98. Hope-not Hobart
99. James Smith[14]

Both the Pilgrims and the Puritans – who came a few years later to open a satellite campus in the Boston area – were followers of John Calvin. Calvinism's core tenets can be summarized by the acronym T.U.L.I.P.

TOTAL DEPRAVITY: The most succinct description yet of adjunct working conditions.

UNCONDITIONAL REJECTION: Job rejections must never include a reason.

LIMITED TENURE: Ideally limited to one or two professors in charge of job rejections.

IRRESISTABLE SNACKS: Offer free donuts once per year to keep adjuncts hooked.

PERSERVERANCE OF THE PRESIDENT: Fire as many adjuncts as necessary to keep senior administrator salaries as high as possible.

The Puritan emphasis on endless labor, chastity, and somber dress naturally produced a society full of adjunct professors. As a result, every now and then they needed to cull the population a bit. When the usual strategies of shaming, banishment, and canceling courses at the last minute weren't enough, the Puritans had one final trick up their sleeves: they simply rebranded adjunct professors as witches.

---

[14]Likely an alias for the well-known adjunct "God-has-tricked-me-into-going-to-grad-school-and-subsequently-exploited-my-labor Johnson."

Fig. 13 Seventeenth-Century Poster Advertising an Adjunct Professor's Teaching Review

Compared to modern academic job interviews, a seventeenth-century witch trial was practically a walk in the park. Being dunked in water? Just a therapeutic cold plunge. Pressed with weights? Shiatsu massage. Burned at the stake? Okay, that one sucks, but at least it's over after twenty minutes or so, while a tenure-track job interview can last *two days*.

Fig. 14. Puritan Academic Job Interview

Of course, most adjunct professors accused of being witches were innocent. Those who were smart enough to make a pact with Satan avoided notice by insisting that the Dark One either grant them tenure or, for those who truly did not value their souls, a cushy role in the university's Human Resources department, hiring, firing, and immolating adjunct professors on a daily basis.

PART FIVE: THE ENLIGHTENMENT

Eventually the age of darkness – shrouded in superstition and ignorance – gave way to an enlightened era, where modern, scientific ideas about which races were better than others began to take hold. This was truly a golden age for adjunct professors. In addition to teaching classes on mathematics, science, and what dinosaurs might have looked like, there were serious improvements to their working conditions. Revolutions in America and France[15] raised adjunct salaries from one stale loaf of bread per week to *one-and-a-half* stale loaves. Moreover, unwanted adjuncts were no longer burned at the stake. They were guillotined instead.

Fig. 15. Firing Adjuncts During the French Revolution

---

[15]In keeping with the Enlightenment's commitment to scientific racism, revolutions in Haiti were not talked about.

PART SIX: THE INDUSTRIAL REVOLUTION

At the same time that the French were devising the most efficient way to cut off people's heads, the English were working on the most efficient way to transform the profits from slavery into profits for factory owners. And thus, the Industrial Revolution was born. Of course, adjuncts did not work in the grueling garment and metalwork factories of Northern England. They did, however, work at universities run by people who looked at these factories and said: let's make our school a lot more like that.

FAMOUS ADJUNCTS IN HISTORY: No. 16

KARL MARX

Probably the best-known critic of both capitalism and the Industrial Revolution, Marx is also remembered for his work on behalf of adjunct professors, famously writing "A specter is haunting Europe – the specter of tenure." Marx himself worked as an adjunct during his time in London. Frequently kicked out of the British Library on account of his awesome beard, Marx was forced to teach community college courses on home economics (a tenured prof taught political economy), which he recounts in his famous book *Das Adjunct* (1867).

Courtesy British Library "Do Not Admit" List

The suffering of adjuncts during the Industrial Revolution was best depicted in the novels of Charles Dickens. While Dickens himself was not an adjunct (in fact, he often used adjuncts to write the last 600 pages of his novels), he nevertheless sympathized with what he called "those luckless and pitiable wretches." Who among us can forget the sad moment when Vice-President of Finance Ebeneezer Scrooge forces Tiny

Tim to grade 75 freshman comp papers before he can have a slice of Christmas goose? Or adjunct professor of Childhood Studies Oliver Twist begging for a second serving of gruel at the faculty holiday party? Or Oliver's friend, Master Bates[16], getting tased and escorted off campus by security guards simply because he told his students his name?

BONUS COMEDY CONTENT: This doesn't have anything to do with academia, but here is a definitive ranking of Charles Dickens novel title anagrams.

10. BANNED SODOMY
9. SOVIET TWIRL
8. FOUL RUM URINATED
7. OILY TUSH ORTHOPEDICS
6. HAKE BLOUSE
5. APE EXCRETING TOAST
4. RANDY BUGBEAR
3. LESBIAN CHICK ONLY
2. SCROTAL CHARISMA
1. TIRED HAMS[17]

---

[16]No need to look it up: yes, "Master Bates" is a real character name, just like Henry James' "Fanny Assingham," or Leo Tolstoy's "Count Jackinoff."
[17]On second thought, the following anagrams actually are about academia: 1, 2, 3, 5, 6, and 8.

CONCLUSION

The history of the adjunct professor did not end in the nineteenth century, of course. Nor did it end in the twentieth century, despite Ronald Reagan's famous "War on Book Learning." To be fair, it probably will end sometime in the twenty-first century, when all universities and colleges will be replaced with Amazon fulfilment centers and AWS servers devoted to pumping out carbon dioxide and A.I.-generated movies about sea creatures that all look and talk like Adam Sandler. But until that day comes, adjunct professors are a fact of life. Like, your life. Because you agreed to become one, remember? And because you chose this career every bad thing that happens to you is 100% your fault, at least according to some assholes on Twitter (and the university's official website). But don't worry, *How to Succeed in Academia* still believes in you! More specifically, we believe you're going to need the following advice to make it through the next eight months without suffering a total mental breakdown or, even worse, writing the LSAT. So read on, friends, and learn what being an adjunct professor today is really like.

How to Overcome Imposter Syndrome When You're Six Raccoons Living in a Fjällräven Parka

Almost everybody in academia experiences imposter syndrome at one point or another. Let this guide help you overcome this significant challenge.

Imposter syndrome is real. In a competitive field like academia, everybody feels like a fraud sometimes, whether it's a scathing peer review, a nasty comment from a student, or being shooed away by campus security when you get caught eating apple cores and chicken bones out of the dining hall dumpster at 3 a.m. The following tips will help you feel like you belong in the Ivory Tower, even when that little voice in your head says, "I'm not good enough," or "Nobody likes me," or "I'm actually half a dozen raccoons nestled inside an abandoned upscale Swedish jacket."

Tell yourself, "My research matters."

So what if your research hasn't been cited by any major scholars? If your research matters to you, it matters, period. And who cares if it's a little unconventional? Or if it isn't really research at all, but a collection of shiny trinkets that you've meticulously washed in a puddle of rainwater behind the library? It's your work, and you need to own it, whether that means standing up to a critical peer reviewer, or fending off a flock of hissing Canada geese who want to steal the cache of apple cores and soggy hot dog buns you've tucked into the pocket of your Arctic Green Nuuk parka/faculty office.

Take student evaluations with a grain of salt.

Student evaluations of your teaching can be helpful, but they can also be quite cruel. Comments about your appearance are especially rough. It's hard to tune out critical remarks about your hair, clothing, or dexterous prehensile forepaws. Let's check out a few sample comments to see if we can read between the lines:

"I can't understand what they're saying."
Sometimes students only hear what they want to hear, and it can be hard for you to push back against those expectations. For example, a student who wants to hear a lecture about biochemistry might find herself challenged by a lecture that is actually just forty-five minutes of chittering, growling, and hissing. (Although studies show that 90 percent of students won't be able to tell the difference anyway.)

"They never take their parka off. Also, I don't think they have a face or hands."
Judgmental comments about your clothing can cut to the quick. Students may not realize that you need that parka to feel safe and warm, and also to create the illusion that you are a single human being with a PhD and a

job instead of a family of nocturnal quadrupeds who are being pursued by local animal-control authorities for urinating in the university president's office (although this could be a gray area if you work as an adjunct professor).

"The professor bit me."
Sounds like you should have kept your goddamn hands off the professor's collection of apple cores then.

Find your voice in faculty meetings.
Speaking up in department meetings can be daunting, especially as a junior faculty member. Sometimes you feel like you shouldn't say anything if you're the youngest person in the room, and this problem is compounded if you only have a life span of two to four years (and that's if you can avoid getting hit by a bus or eating hot dog buns laced with rat poison). If a tenured colleague shoots down one of your ideas, stay calm and clearly explain where you are coming from. And if that doesn't work, crawl up their pant leg and start nibbling and scratching until they run out of the room screaming and/or agree to your proposed changes to the first-year survey course.

Remember: Everybody has bad days.
There isn't a professor alive who hasn't discovered that they just taught a class with chalk dust on their back, an open fly, or a peanut butter jar stuck on their head. Learn to brush it off, to zip it up, and to use your hind legs to dislodge your skull from the jar's narrow opening before campus security can tase you and dump you, the rest of your family, and the tattered remains of your Fjällräven parka in a Salvation Army donation bin.

Embrace having a Plan B.
Sometimes a job in academia just isn't for you, so it's always good to think about an "alt-ac" career. Evaluate your skill set. If you're good at writing and critical thinking, maybe you should consider law school. And if you're good at sifting through garbage cans for free food, sleeping

during the day, and hissing at your rivals, you're already 99 percent of the way toward a career as a freelance writer.

How to Finish All Your Grading Using Nothing but Time Management and This Cursed Tibetan Monkey's Paw

Getting grading done on time is a huge challenge for ANY professor! Let these useful tips help you get yours finished as quickly as possible.

Block Out Distractions

Grading is tough work under the best of circumstances, so you don't want to deal with distractions on top of all that marking. Find a quiet place to get down to work, such as a cozy nook in your apartment, a quiet table at your favorite café, or a haunted antique store dealing exclusively in exotic and esoteric relics from the ancient Far East.

Establish Goals and Priorities

When you have a huge amount of work on your plate it can be tough to get started. A good strategy is to break everything down and set achievable daily goals to prioritize what matters most. Grading two hundred essays in one day is impossible, but grading twenty essays per day for the next ten days could be achievable. Likewise, simply declaring yourself to be "Grand Emperor and Sex God" of your university is unlikely to do anything, but wishing for it using the pinkie finger of a cursed Tibetan monkey's paw can help you achieve your goal in as little time as it takes for a five-hundred-year-old baboon finger to curl into a tight, mummified fist.

Set Reasonable Time Limits

Taking on a new position can be exciting, but it also runs the risk of overwhelming you with new tasks and information. Making the leap from grad student to adjunct professor can have this effect, as can transitioning from being an adjunct professor to becoming your university's first Grand

Emperor and Sex God. The number of meetings senior administrators need to attend can be something of a culture shock, as can the daily human sacrifices and orgies that are part and parcel of being a living deity and fertility idol. You're going to need to be protective of your sleep time (8 hours per night) and hydration needs (25-30 gallons of Gatorade per hour). Maybe a penthouse apartment (with unlimited Gatorade) would help? Just talk to the monkey's paw (*ring finger curls*).

Be Flexible

Like, physically. These orgies are brutal for your sciatica. Of course, the monkey's paw can help with that (*middle finger curls*).

Learn to Say No

You've got to remember to make time for yourself, and in academia the "asks" just keep on coming. Join this committee, review this paper, preside over this cannibalistic battle royale in the quad with your close friend Dionysius. There's only so much you can cram into a workday. If you have to say "no" every now and then, what's the worst that can happen? Somebody else has to sit on a committee? Dionysius will behead the university President and wear his face as a mask? Oh shit, that's going to be a bit of a problem with the Board of Governors. Better wind back the clock (*index finger curls*).

Reward Yourself

Sure, you're an all-powerful Grand Emperor and Sex God who palls around with all the coolest demigods, but you still need a little reward from time to time. Two words: Häagen. Dazs. But they're out of your favorite flavor at the campus store! Ah well, I guess this is the only option (*thumb curls*).

Finish What You Started

Turns out that between the ritualistic sacrifices, endless orgies, and premium ice cream, you forgot to do any of your grading. And now your monkey's paw is basically just a paperweight. Maybe you should have read some time management books before you burned down the library during last week's wine-fueled Bacchanal?

Quit

You're no longer a living God and you can't make rent or afford to eat. But at least that grading is somebody else's problem now.

PROFILES IN FAILURE:
I Drank From The Wrong Holy Grail And Now I'm An Adjunct Professor Of Comparative Literature

I was on vacation with the wife and kids. A week away from the office, not checking my messages, spending all day by the pool. Real nice time. Last day of the trip and I'm craving a Starbucks. I leave the hotel to look for one, but before I know it, I'm lost and standing in front of this gigantic building carved out of a rock. Some kind of ancient temple. It's probably got a Starbucks. I step inside.

There's an old guy standing there dressed like a medieval knight. I figure he must be the barista. I ask him for a Kiwi Starfruit Lemonade, and he just stares at me. Okay fine. So I ask him what he does have to drink, and he leads me to a room filled with cups and a big bowl of water. He points to the cups and says, "You must choose wisely." I spot a bunch of skeletons in the corner, and I ask him what happened to those guys, and he says, "They chose poorly." I'm starting to regret not just getting a Jamba Juice back at the hotel.

The cups all look really old and gross. But then I spot a metal water bottle. It's blue and white and says SUNY BUFFALO on the side. I reach for it, and I can see the old guy starts to try to stop me, but he holds off. A single tear rolls down his cheek.

I grab the bottle, fill it up, and take a drink. The old guy looks me right in the eyes and says, "You chose very poorly." I take another sip.

I blink, and suddenly I'm standing in front of a room of college kids. Most of them are sleeping on their backpacks. I'm talking about some guy named Alain Robbe-Grillet and telling everybody that their essays were due three weeks ago. I look at the blackboard and it says COMP LIT 101. I feel more afraid than I ever have in my life.

I hear the old guy's voice in my head. He says that I have to work as an adjunct professor for the rest of eternity or until I get a tenure-track job, whichever comes first. I try to scream, but the only thing that comes out is a forty-five-minute lecture about something called "le Nouveau Roman."

It's not all bad. I like Buffalo wings, and the Bills are pretty good this season. Sure, I'm grading five hundred papers a week and living in a 1990 Honda Civic, but at least I get to hold my office hours in the campus Starbucks. I can't afford anything off the menu, but one of the baristas gives me a nice cup of ice water if I agree to stop asking customers if they've seen a medieval knight wandering around town. I know it's a long shot, but I figure if I'm going to break this curse I have a much better chance of tracking down a 1,200-year-old French knight in downtown Buffalo than I do of actually landing a tenure-track job.

ACADEMIC GLOSSARY[18]

Office Hours: While the criminal justice system sentences offenders to jail time, academia – despite objections from the United Nations Human Rights Council – condemns adjunct professors to hours and hours of unpaid time in a basement office. Unlike death row prisoners who have a cell to themselves, adjuncts must share their office space with dozens of others, many of whom have been sentenced for such serious offences as applying for a tenure-track job, asking for a raise, or stealing another adjunct's leftover (but nevertheless delicious) baked potato from Wendy's.

Teaching Load: Much like a pickup truck's payload, a "teaching load" is the maximum amount of teaching an adjunct can handle before some part of them is permanently damaged. Unlike a pickup truck, adjunct professors do not come with any kind of manufacturer's warranty, so worn-out models are immediately sent to the scrap yard (i.e., Wendy's).

Grading Deadline: The line, usually estimated as one hundred essays per day, beyond which grading can result in instant death, or at the very least, an unpaid break at Wendy's.

Baconator: A half pound of fresh, never frozen, ground beef, two slices of American cheese, six strips of applewood bacon, Heinz ketchup, mayonnaise, all served on a fluffy, freshly baked bun. It's delicious! It's also the only thing (other than a tenure-track job) that will get adjuncts to kill one another. Just drop one of these in that shared office and watch the carnage begin.

---

[18] Brought to you by Wendy's®! Wendy's: Home of the Baconator (and the Adjunct Professor).

CHAPTER V:
Getting A Tenure-Track Job

This page intentionally left blank

CHAPTER ~~V~~ VI:
~~Getting A Tenure-Track Job~~
Still Working As An Adjunct Professor

It's probably occurred to you by this point that you're not going to get a tenure-track job. If that *hasn't* crossed your mind, a) your employer is doing an amazing job of brainwashing you, seriously, props to them, and b) you might want to flip back to Chapter One and start reading all over again.[19] Because we've been clear about this from the beginning: tenure-track jobs don't exist. It's best to think of them as a kind of mythical creature, like a unicorn (rare), bigfoot (the subject of extensive searches), or leprechaun (there might be one in Ireland).

If you're going to make a career out of being an adjunct professor, you're going to need some support. This chapter has got you covered! Or rather, it has the people in your life that you need to support you covered! In these pages they will find thoughtful and helpful tips that will make *your* life better. So please, share these wise words with them. All you need to do is buy, let's say, two dozen additional copies of *How to Succeed in Academia*, give them to people you care about, and ask them to reimburse[20] you. We're thinking friends, family, or really anybody who you can track down and pester until they agree to Venmo you twenty dollars. Cast a wide net! If you need to order more than two dozen copies of this book, please know that we support that too (emotionally, not financially – that's up to you).

---

[19]Better yet, buy another copy of this book and start reading that instead. Honestly, if you've been following these instructions, you should own 10-12 copies of this book by now, one for each adjunct you share an office with (don't give away your copies to them, though – those jerks need to buy their own).

[20]We realize most adjunct professors will be unfamiliar with this word, so here is a brief definition: Reimburse (verb): to repay a sum of money that has been spent. Crazy shit, we know.

Board Games for Adjunct Professors

Even adjunct professors need to relax sometimes. Next time you see one of the adjuncts in your life, propose playing these fun board games with them – they'll be sure to thank you!

Settlers of Catan

On an island with scarce resources, you are quickly isolated in a barren desert (the academic job market). A robber steals your laptop, the sandwich you brought from home to avoid spending money you don't have on campus, and all of your bricks. Your attempt to exchange three sheep for a tenure-track job is unsuccessful.

Monopoly

Rents are skyrocketing in your city, even though adjunct salaries have been frozen at $200 since 1935. You are forced to move from St. James Place to Baltic Avenue. A surprise second-place showing in a local beauty contest provides temporary relief, but an academic conference at Marvin Gardens wipes out your savings. Your friends (a thimble, a top hat, and a Scottish Terrier) tell you that you should have invested in railroads and utilities when you had the chance. You decide that it would be easier to just wait out the rest of the game in jail.

The Game of Life

You live in a car. The car is also your office.

Hungry Hungry Hippos

You and three of the twelve people you share an office with are competing for a limited number of marbles (job interviews). You get the most interviews, but you have to put $2,000 on your credit card to actually go to them. Eventually, all of the job searches are canceled. You ask your landlord if he will accept marbles for rent. He will not. You tell yourself that you will only play the game one more time, and then you're going to law school. You play five more times.

Risk

You move to Mongolia for a postdoc, but it is suddenly invaded by Japan. Running for your life, you eventually make it to Siberia. You are told that, unfortunately, your postdoc cannot be transferred to a different territory. You discover vodka. You get a job at the Pizza Hut in Omsk. You do not notice when Quebec conquers the entire planet.

Clue

A murder has been committed and you know that your dissertation supervisor (Professor Plum) is the culprit. You can't say anything since you still need his letters of recommendation. You let Colonel Mustard take the fall, telling yourself that it's okay since he is part of the military industrial complex (your supervisor would like that). You never ask your supervisor why he thought it would be a good idea to bludgeon someone to death in the faculty lounge with a candlestick.

Operation

Surprise! You need to sell a kidney to pay the interest on your student loans.

Jenga

You build an ivory tower out of wooden blocks. Just for fun, you start removing crucial parts of the tower's foundation. You notice that the tower is becoming increasingly precarious. Instead of replacing the stuff you took away, you just take more and more until the whole mess comes tumbling down. Congratulations, you are now a university administrator.

MARIE CURIE

Marie Curie is remembered today for her discovery of two elements, for coining the term "radioactivity," for being the first woman to win a Nobel Prize, and for being the first person to win *two* Nobel Prizes. But all of that pales in comparison to her greatest achievement: she was the first – and, as of this writing, only – person to move from an adjunct to a tenure-track professorship at the same university, which she accomplished at the University of Paris on July 3rd, 1934, exactly one day before she died from exposure to radiation caused by her many years as an underpaid lab tech/custodian.

Courtesy Swedish Academy Part-Time Faculty Page

Back-To-School Supplies for Adjunct Professors

Back-to-school supplies aren't just for students! The adjunct professor in your life needs some new SWAG too. Consider this a shopping list!

Backpack

Should be large enough to hold a twelve-year-old laptop, a cubic foot of ungraded freshman comp papers, and the four yogurt cups that will be your only form of sustenance during the fifteen hours you will spend on campus today. Bonus points if the backpack is soft enough to double as a pillow, punching bag, or non-judgmental sleeping companion when you pass out on your twin size futon every night.

Tissues

Always handy if you get a case of the sniffles, or if you need to weep in the hallway in front of your students and colleagues after receiving yet another tenure-track job rejection. Can also be bartered for additional yogurt cups.

Pencil case

Try to find something spacious, so you can stock it with fun supplies like colored pencils and plastic scissors, and also so nobody will notice when you start filling it with the turkey wraps you're stealing from a departmental reception you weren't invited to. If anybody does catch you in the act, try bribing them with one of your yogurt cups. If they refuse your bribe, threaten them with a sharpened colored pencil as you slowly back out of the room. You may experience a rush of adrenaline as you commit this minor criminal transgression. This is good. Chase that feeling.

Ballpoint pens

These have several uses:
- Grading
- Taking attendance
- Writing your name on your yogurt cups
- A makeshift weapon to be brandished if another adjunct tries to steal one of your yogurt cups, as once again the forbidden thrill of criminal behavior sets your soul on fire

New clothes

You've spent all your money on yogurt cups and colored pencils, so a flashy new outfit is clearly out of the question. Maybe try repurposing some of your old clothes instead? Use your plastic scissors to cut eye and mouth holes in an old sweatpant leg and — *voila!* — you've got a brand-new mask. Now put on the mask and walk to the nearest bank.

Notebook

You used to pass notes to your friends all the time in high school, so why not try it again? Rip out a sheet of crisp, lined paper and write a brief note explaining that you've got a bomb in your backpack and that the bank teller should give you $500,000 in unmarked, non-consecutive bills. Make sure to include one of those fun Y/N checkboxes so the teller can answer you in secret!

Lunchbox

There are so many cool designs to choose from, but you'll be fine with any lunch box that can comfortably hold at least 12 lbs worth of $100 U.S. banknotes.

Bus pass

You'll need this pass to commute between the three campuses where you teach for less than minimum wage. It will also come in handy when you need to disappear from a busy city street, highjack a bus full of passengers, and get to the airport before the SWAT team can be mobilized.

Post-its

These are always useful, but never more so than when you're holed up in a private jet with twenty hostages who all think you have a bomb in your backpack. There's no easier way to send a quick message to the FBI negotiators on the runway, or to the pilot, who you order to fly you to an undisclosed Central American location or you will threaten to detonate what are, in fact, several dozen midterms that your students failed to collect during your office hours.

Oceanside villa

This is really more of a "nice to have" instead of a "need to have," but you've worked hard, paid your dues, landed on INTERPOL's Most Wanted List, and you deserve a treat. You recline in your hammock, watching the Pacific waves crash against the sandy shore, and open one of your favorite yogurt cups. The yogurt reminds you of your teaching days, but you tell yourself that you can never go back to that life, not least because you will be sent to a Supermax prison the second you set foot on U.S. soil. No adjunct professorship is worth that. But you do have a plastic surgeon and a human smuggler on speed dial just in case your former school is ever hiring a tenure-track professor. Pulling off the crime of the century is one thing, but landing a tenure-track job in the same department where you worked as an adjunct would be an actual miracle.

Fig. 16. Behind the Numbers: Adjunct Professor Hobbies

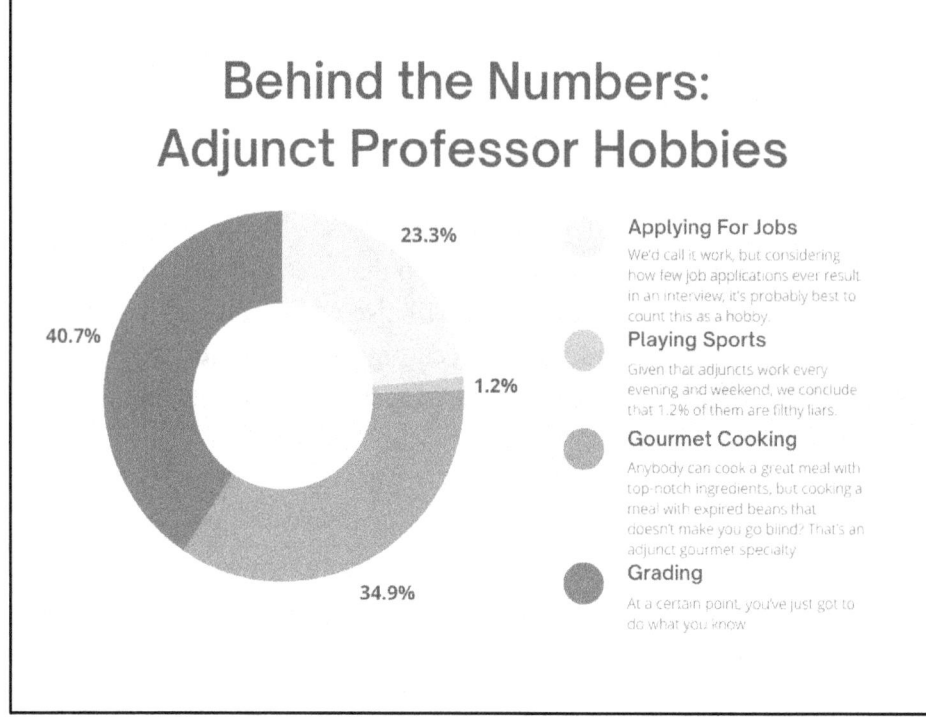

Classic Video Games for Adjunct Professors

Everybody needs to relax at the end of a long day, and that includes adjunct professors. So why not propose playing a video game with them? They can't afford new games, so it's considered polite to stick to the classics.

Mario Kart

You and the seven other members of your grad school cohort are competing for the last tenure-track job in the Mushroom Kingdom. It's a standard interview: meet with the committee, give a job talk, and drive around in a go-kart, hurling turtle shells at the other candidates. You get off to a great start, holding down first place as you zip around campus, carefully avoiding undergrads, banana peels, and probing questions about your personal life from the oldest professor on the hiring committee. After taking out one of your rivals with a red turtle shell — and a devastating critique of their reading of Deleuze — you suddenly find yourself in a scary new part of campus. It's a dark room, filled with wailing ghosts and holes in the rickety wooden floor that reveal a bottomless abyss of despair. You are told that this is the part-time faculty office. You are also told that the tenure-track job search has been canceled and that the best they can offer you is a one-semester adjunct contract, a shared desk in the ghost office, and a salary of two banana peels per month. You will not be reimbursed for your go-kart expenses.

Ms. Pac-Man

You live in the labyrinthine world of the academic job market, pursued at all times by four haunting specters: Inky, Blinky, Pinky, and Student Loan Debt. You stay alive by stealing pieces of fruit, selling "power pellets" to undergrads cramming for the LSAT, and by teaching six sections of freshman comp every semester. Each time you think you find your way out of the maze, it turns out to be a tunnel that leads you back to where you were 10 years and 800 job applications ago. When the ghosts finally catch up with you, you ask if they would mind calling you "Doctor" instead of "Ms." They frown, tell you to stop being so pushy, then eat you alive.

Donkey Kong

You try to climb to the top of the Ivory Tower, but you face all the usual obstacles: a lack of tenure-track job openings, the glacial pace of academic publishing, and a giant fucking gorilla who throws heavy wooden barrels at you. You try everything: jumping, smashing the barrels with a hammer, and writing a lengthy Twitter thread about tenured primates' bad behavior in the academy. You get a lot of retweets, but you also get hit with a barrel while you're checking your phone. You plummet from the Ivory Tower and are never heard from again. The gorilla is promoted to VP of Barrel Outreach and Innovation.

Tetris

Your life is a complicated puzzle. You try to arrange the various pieces of your academic career into a seamless 100-hour work week: there's a "T" for teaching, an "S" for students, a "Z" for Zoom meetings, and a "J" for your job at Quiznos, which actually provides the bulk of your income. Before long, everything piles up, and it's game over. You hit reset on academia, but stick with Quiznos because the employee discount on toasted subs is the closest thing you've ever had to a retirement plan.

Paperboy

Unable to afford a bus pass, you steal a bike from a frat house and ride around town, returning all the essays your students never bothered to pick up. You zip through the student neighborhoods near campus, deftly avoiding abandoned kegs, pools of vomit, and eye contact with anyone who might be sober enough to recognize you. You're doing great — you might even get home in time to do more grading! — until a sophomore business major runs you over with the "spare" BMW his parents let him borrow for the school year. Your injuries are minor, but since your university hasn't provided adjuncts with health insurance since the 1970s, you are forced to spend six months convalescing on your basement apartment futon after your homemade plaster cast gives you a staph infection. The university assigns your classes/paper route to a fresh-faced Ph.D. grad, and you spend your days trying to buy expired antibiotics on the dark web.

Super Mario Bros.

You successfully avoid man-eating plants, flying turtles, and a fire-breathing dragon to arrive on time for your interview with Princess Toadstool, only to be told that it's actually being held in another castle. Waiting for an Uber to take you across town to a different lava-filled fortress, you begin to seriously consider an alt-ac career in the plumbing industry.

Minecraft

Getting Started

First, you need to decide between Creative Mode and Survival Mode. In Creative Mode, you are like a god, the lord and master of all you see, with an infinite number of items and resources at your disposal. Creative Mode is only available for tenured professors. Everybody else has to play in Survival Mode. You will also need to choose a difficulty level. Your options are Peaceful, Easy, Normal, Hard, and Adjunct Professor. Let's select that last one and see what happens.

Your Character Spawns

Your character could spawn in any biome, but since you selected Adjunct Professor Mode, there is a 90 percent chance you will appear in the bathroom of a Subway restaurant where you are grading essays using a malfunctioning hand dryer as a desk and trying to answer panicky student emails on a nine-year-old iPhone. If you chose to begin with a Bonus Chest, it should be in one of the adjacent bathroom stalls. Look inside to find useful items that will help you on your quest, including more essays to grade, half a meatball sub, and a PhD in the History of Consciousness from UC Santa Cruz.

Building a Shelter

You can build your shelter out of almost any material but choose something cozy since you'll be sharing your shelter/house/office/classroom/occasional Airbnb with every other adjunct professor playing in your realm. A well-built shelter will keep the elements and most hostile mobs at bay, but letters from student loan collection agencies will always find you. Don't bother crafting windows for your shelter, since it must be located underground next to a lava pool, a bottomless chasm, and several broken photocopiers.

Searching for Resources

Start by gathering valuable natural resources such as wood, cobblestone, and coal, all of which can be bartered with villagers for the Chobani yogurt cups that will constitute 90 percent of your diet (the other 10 percent comes from the meatball sub you found in the Subway bathroom, so eat it sparingly). You should also gather sticks and wool to craft the futon that will be your bed, office, and occasional sexual partner. If you encounter gold, diamonds, or anything else even remotely valuable, immediately select SAVE AND QUIT and invest your newfound wealth into minting NFTs of your negative Rate My Professor evaluations.

Crafting Supplies

Combine four wooden planks to create a crafting table. You can use this helpful item to craft pretty much anything, including powerful weapons, armor, and tools. Unfortunately, you can also use it as a desk, and since you have two hundred essays on gender identity in *Jane Eyre* to grade before tomorrow morning, you'd better get started. The good news is that you don't need to sleep in *Minecraft*, so this can be just like one of your real-life workdays. Only stop working if you need to barter for more Chobanis, if a zombie starts trying to eat you, or—worst of all—if a zombie tries to close SpeedGrader before you can save all the comments on those essays.

Encountering Hostile Mobs

Zombies, spiders, and creepers will all try to kill you, but the most dangerous hostile mob you will encounter is the dreaded "hiring committee," who will not only kill you but also demand that you give them a CV, a cover letter, academic transcripts from undergrad, grad school, and kindergarten, seven letters of reference, a twelve-year research plan, and three thousand dollars (or the equivalent in Chobani yogurt cups) to pay your own way to an on-campus interview.

Fighting the Ender Dragon

To reach the end of the game, you will need to fight the most terrifying, powerful, and remorseless enemy you can imagine. His name is Ben Peterson, and he was granted tenure in 1978 with one conference paper and zero publications on his CV. Despite getting his first tenure-track job because his supervisor was a drinking buddy of the department chair, he now expects all job applicants to have three books (with a fourth under contract) by the time they finish graduate school. He has published one book in forty-five years and made $325,000 last year. Conventional weapons (like peer review) cannot harm him, so your only hope is to say good things about him and pray that he gets offered a job as a university president in another state.

Starting Over

Playing *Minecraft* on Adjunct Professor Mode means you will need to start a new game from scratch every eight to twelve weeks. Your progress will not be saved, because according to the university's HR department, it does not exist. You might want to consider playing a game that simulates a safer and more stable career, such as auto thief, soldier of fortune, or assassin. However, given the large number of new adjunct professors joining the game each year, the smartest move might be selling your gaming system and funneling the profits into Chobani yogurt stock.

Christmas Presents for Adjunct Professors

This holiday season you may have to purchase a present for the adjunct professor in your life. This guide lets you know which gifts adjunct professors will appreciate the most.

Ugly Sweater

A garish Rudolph the Red-Nosed Reindeer sweater (with a real light bulb nose) is great for a laugh at holiday parties with friends and family. But for an adjunct professor, Rudolph's glowing nose can also provide much-needed illumination (and warmth) when reading the Academic Jobs Wiki while home alone on Christmas Eve after the power and heat have been cut off in their studio apartment. As a bonus, this inexpensive and highly flammable sweater can serve as a fast-acting fire starter if they decide to burn down the collection agency that's been hounding them over the credit card debt they racked up in grad school.

Socks

Socks might seem like a boring present, but any enterprising adjunct professor can turn a sock into a mitten, a tiny pillow, a pencil case, or — when filled with pebbles from the campus parking lot — a rudimentary club that can be used to mug the university president on his way home from a fundraiser with wealthy alumni.

Lump of Coal

This classic stocking stuffer lets everybody know who you think is on Santa's "naughty" list. It also makes the adjunct professor in your life think that you have read their recent journal article on literary representations of working conditions in Victorian coal mines (even though, like any sane person, you do not read academic journal articles for fun). At the same time, a lump of coal can provide minutes and minutes of valuable warmth in the unheated basement office that they share with a dozen other adjuncts, a family of possums, and several hundred square feet of asbestos.

Tree Trimmings

Is there anything more fun than making a festive wreath out of the trimmings from your Christmas tree? How about making several dozen wreaths, draping them over a warm photocopier in a seldom-traveled university hallway, and napping/quietly weeping inside this woodland nest during a rare break in a 14-hour teaching day? Does that sound like fun? No? Just hand over the garbage bag full of twigs, asshole.

All the Cheese in Your Refrigerator

Hey, remember when you went to the bathroom ten minutes ago? That was also when the adjunct professor you invited over stole all the cheese in your refrigerator. They'll eat some of it themselves; the rest will be bartered with other adjuncts for lumps of coal. If you want to provide a special treat, purchase a 24-slice pack of Kraft Singles, which your adjunct professor friend can use either as Post-its or a rudimentary advent calendar. Each day is more delicious than the last.

Your Credit Cards

Hey, remember when that adjunct professor stole all your cheese? Turns out they also stole all the credit cards from your wallet as well. You won't be able to track them down at the university, unfortunately, since they just sent a resignation email from your new iPhone, which they also stole.

Your Passport and Social Security Card

Those too, I'm afraid.

Instant Pot

All that stolen cheese isn't going to melt itself.

Your Identity

You've had a good run. Nice job, nice house, nice family. You went to university for four years, not 14. And now "you" have absconded to an undisclosed foreign location with a low cost of living and shockingly lax international extradition laws. Now that the adjunct professor you were foolish enough to befriend has stolen your identity, you have no choice but to assume theirs. You're going to have to start using phrases like "discursive construct" and "I heard there are free bagels here" in everyday conversations. You're going to have to learn how to grade 300 papers while loitering in a crowded Taco Bell. And, most importantly, you're going to have to make some rich friends who are dumb enough to trust you around their credit cards.

Quiz: Should I Leave Academia?

Question 1: Would you like to make more than $15,000 per year?
   a) I'll be making more than that once I get a tenure-track job
   b) Who cares? I want to do what I love
   c) But I've already spent so much time preparing for this career
   d) YOU'RE GODDAMN RIGHT

ANSWER KEY: D. We only need a single question for this one. If you want to make more money, you have to leave academia. If you want to make *a lot* more money you're going to need a time machine. You've already burned 15 years on this nonsense, you think someone's about to offer you MBA or lawyer money? Let's be real. You're not going to make six figures. But you're not going to make four figures either (as was the case for three of the past five years). You're headed for the bottom third of five-figure territory, baby!

CHAPTER VII:
Leaving Academia

Like an over-educated Rapunzel, you need to escape from the Ivory Tower (you also need a haircut). But unlike Rapunzel, this isn't going to be as simple as throwing yourself out the window.[21] You need a plan. Luckily, once again, *How to Succeed in Academia* has you covered. After 10+ years in academia, you're going to need to acclimate to the real world. This will involve some work stuff, like applying for jobs that don't require you to have a PhD, and some social stuff, like attending parties that require you to shut the fuck up about your PhD. These changes can be tricky – imagine *not* asking a stranger where they went to grad school! – but you can do it.

And so, without further ado, here is our comprehensive guide to working outside of academia, written by someone who hasn't had a real job since 2003.

Editing Your ~~Curriculum Vitae~~Resume

Although these terms are technically interchangeable, for the most part academics have a "curriculum vitae," while normal people have a "resume." And now that you are – in theory, at least – a normie too, you will need to make the switch. There are some crucial differences between the two documents. For starters, a resume is a brief, 1-2 page synopsis of your top qualifications and relevant experience, while a C.V. is a comprehensive list of every mistake you've made in your life, starting with the mistake you made back in Chapter II when you decided to go to grad school. You're going to need to cut a lot, and not just to make things more concise. While having a PhD on a C.V. is a basic requirement to

---

[21] Although now that we think about it, it *can* be that simple.

apply for an academic job, on a normal person's resume it is a red flag on par with a bumper sticker of Calvin peeing on a COVID vaccine.Believe it or not, many employers will see a PhD on your resume and assume that you – a person who made $8,000 last year and sleeps on two bean bag chairs – are "overqualified" for their job. So even though you sacrificed your 20s, early 30s, and your last remaining shreds of dignity to earn a PhD, you're going to need it off your resume. Of course, that *does* leave an otherwise unexplained 5-15 year gap in your work history. But don't worry about it, a solution is at hand! Here is a list of alternate explanations for your PhD years that will make a better impression on potential employers than admitting that you have a doctorate:

- **Prison:** I don't know if you've noticed this, but the United States *loves* putting people in prison. In fact, there's a pretty good chance you're reading this book in prison right now (if so, please re-read the "How to Use this Book" section at the start of this book). Thanks to the magic of the 13th Amendment, many ~~forced laborers~~ prisoners gain invaluable work experience during their sentence, often earning dozens of dollars per year. I know what you're thinking: you already had a job that paid you dozens of dollars *per month*, so why lie about it? The answer is simple: some employers will feel that prisoners deserve a second chance. This is not a feeling people have about underemployed introverts with PhDs in Renaissance Poetry. So start editing that resume and working on your homemade tattoos (think tear drops and Roman numerals, not literary quotations and illustrations from *Charlotte's Web*). You're an ex-con now!

- **Fugue State:** You'd be amazed by what a fugue state can do for your credibility. The beauty of the fugue state is that you don't *choose* it. It chooses you. And therefore, you can't be held responsible for it.[22] This means that an employer will view a fugue state as an unfortunate twist of fate, rather than, say, a conscious decision to spend 12 years studying the semiotics of

---

[22]Legal disclaimer: This probably isn't true, but who really knows? Maybe you can write the LSAT and figure this out for us.

Super Bowl halftime shows, or whatever else you were able to convince a committee of professors to let you "research."

- **CIA Black Site:** It's not like you need to be guilty of anything to take advantage of this excuse. After all, the whole point of a CIA Black Site is that it gives the government somewhere to torture and imprison people *without* due process. Maybe your license plate accidentally contained the characters "05AMA" and that was all they needed to pick you up for a brisk eight years of waterboarding and sleep deprivation. That could happen to anybody! While spending those same eight years grading essays in your parents' basement could really only happen to you.

- **Lost In the Woods:** This happens more than you would think. Somebody is hiking the Appalachian Trail, goes fifty yards into the woods to take a pee, and can't find their way back. Next thing you know, it's ten years later and they've been surviving on squirrel thighs and rainwater (which, for what it's worth, is nutritionally indistinguishable from the average adjunct diet). A couple of photoshopped news stories about your inspiring tale of survival and eventual rescue will be enough for most employers. Just be aware that they will almost certainly tap you to organize any kind of outdoorsy "team building" activities.

- **Witness Protection Program:** Explaining to an employer that you were a professor who made less money than a twelve-year-old paperboy is challenging. So why not just say that you were an accountant for the Irish Mob instead? Nobody will understand if you say you were motivated by a desire to teach *Moby-Dick* to a room full of bored undergraduates. But they will totally understand if you say you were motivated by a desire to turn state's witness before a guy named Connell could break both your arms.

- **Medically Induced Coma:** This is close to the truth, so if you want to play it safe, just say you suffered a catastrophic brain injury. Again: this is basically what happened anyway, so it really shouldn't be that hard to pull off.

"Alt-Ac" Careers

If you're thinking about leaving academia you will inevitably encounter the term "alt-ac." The "alt" stands for "alternative," and the "ac" represents the sound of your PhD being violently regurgitated, although in this case the "hairball" is a modest job you could have got with a bachelor's degree 12 years ago. For academic administrators who rely on a never-ending stream of ~~fresh victims~~ graduate students, an "alternative academic career" is a great way to rebrand not being able to get a job as a professor and needing a Plan B before the credit card companies figure out where you're hiding. To be clear: the author of this book 100% supports anybody leaving academia for a real job. This is a good thing, and more people should do it. But most real jobs don't require a PhD, nor should they. But there has been a recent trend of PhD programs claiming that new students know they won't get a tenure-track job, but they want to get a PhD anyway to help get an "alt-ac" job, which again, by definition, is a job that does not require a PhD. This is a bit like using your PhD in physics to build a super-powerful laser rifle and then shooting yourself in the balls with it. Okay, maybe it's not like that (who the hell understands how physics works?), but it's still not a good idea. Almost everybody who gets a PhD does so because a) they want to be a professor, or b) they don't know what else to do with their life. Pretty much nobody gets a PhD because they want to wait nine years to get a job they are already qualified for. Again, anybody who bails on academia to get a job like that is doing the right thing. But pretending that was the plan all along is kind of delusional, which… now that we think about it, is actually a pretty good fit for academia. Never mind!

Goodbye, Academia

And now, friends, we must bid you farewell as you leave the Ivory Tower to pursue your exciting new career doing whatever the fuck pays more than $9/hour. In parting, we offer you the following traditional adjunct professor goodbyes:

- Hold that bus door! HOLD THAT FUCKING BUS DO–

- See you later, bestie! [spoken to a broken vending machine]
- I'll pay you back next week.
- I'll pay you back next month.
- I borrowed money? Whoa, sorry, I must have been in a fugue state.[23]
- I'll see you at the _____! [literally any event with an open bar]
- You got the first tenure-track job you applied for? That's awesome, I'm so happy for you! Can't wait to hear all about it!
- I'll be there soon. I just need to finish the last of this grading.

---

[23] As should be clear by now, this is a highly versatile excuse.

ACKNOWLEDGMENTS

Thanks to Brian Boone and Marty Dundics of Humorist Books for not getting mad at me when I turned this book in ten months later than when I said I would. It was academia-themed performance art, I swear.

A huge thank you to Chris Monks of *McSweeney's Internet Tendency* for patiently rejecting all the terrible comedy writing I submitted before I finally figured out that making fun of academia was kind of my thing. Everybody in the online comedy world already knows that Chris is a generous and patient editor, but just in case you missed the memo: Chris is great. You should make his life harder by sending him your unedited, 5,000-word personal essay as a .pdf attachment. He loves that stuff!

Caitlin Kunkel is an excellent teacher and writing coach, in addition to being a talented and hilarious writer. This book would not have progressed beyond me wishing it into existence if it wasn't for Caitlin's comedy book proposal class and her careful coaching and editing. Thank you as well to Emma Brodie for an excellent class on pitching agents and writing cover letters.

Thanks to Taylor Kay Phillips, Carlos Greaves, and all the other folks I've met in the comedy writing world who have been supportive of this project. A special thanks to Gary M. Almeter for asking me to co-host a podcast with him. Gary's a great guy, a lot of fun to talk to, and thanks to his generous invitation to join him, I was able to meet many of my comedy writing heroes. He is also the only person who hates condiments more than me, which I deeply respect.

I'm grateful for my friends, both in and outside academia, who've read my stuff and tolerated my jokes: Stirling Prentice, Teresa Smith, Gregory Brophy, Dana Broadbent, Mike Lee, Caroline Herbert, Emily Adrian, Dan Schillinger, Peter Sanagan, Alia Hussey, Tyler Lockyer, Bernadette Smith, Peter Brown, Ali Qadeer, Michelle Miller: thank you.

Thanks to my parents, Mike and Jeanne, for introducing me to a lot of what I've found funny over the years. Thanks to my brother, Terry, for making fun of Mom and Dad with me.

Thank you to Jud, Nancy, and Peter for welcoming me into your family, and for not complaining when I throw out expired food items (especially condiments).

The biggest thank you of all is for my family: my partner, Kate, and our children, Leo and Cora. The three of you are supportive, loving, and surprisingly tolerant of living with a 47-year-old man who thinks he is funny. I love you.

And finally, I'm grateful to many of the folks I've met in academia who, despite what you might have read in this book, are terrific and supportive people. As for certain other people I've met in academia (and whose names are redacted): thanks for the material!

ABOUT THE AUTHOR

Ross Bullen is a writer, an English professor, and a disgruntled former employee of a small-town Renaissance Faire. Since 2010 he has been teaching off – at times *way* off – the tenure-track. Ross has written numerous scholarly essays, delivered dozens of academic papers to audiences large and small (okay, mostly small), and received over 100 tenure-track job rejections, each one of which he cherishes like one of his children. (No offense to his two actual children, with whom he lives in Toronto, along with his partner, Kate).

      Ross has published comedy in *McSweeney's* and *Points in Case,* and has written essays for *The Public Domain Review, American Literature*, and elsewhere. He co-hosts *The Official Dream Dinner Party Podcast* with Gary M. Almeter, where he gets to talk shop – and dinner – with some of today's leading comedy writers.

www.ingramcontent.com/pod-product-compliance
Lightning Source LLC
Chambersburg PA
CBHW061701120626
46550CB00003B/1045